The
Jefferson
Scandals
A REBUTTAL

ALSO BY VIRGINIUS DABNEY

Across the Years: Memories of a Virginian
Richmond: The Story of a City
Virginia: The New Dominion
The Patriots (editor)
Dry Messiah: The Life of Bishop Cannon
Below the Potomac
Liberalism in the South
Virginia Commonwealth University: A Sesquicentennial History
Pistols and Pointed Pens: The Duelling Editors of Old Virginia
Virginius Dabney's Virginia: Writings About the Old Dominion
The Last Review: The Confederate Reunion, Richmond, 1932
Mr. Jefferson's University: A History

Rembrandt Peale's Thomas Jefferson, painted in 1800, the year of his first election to the presidency, and considered the best portrait of him.

The Jefferson Scandals

A REBUTTAL

by Virginius Dabney

Lanham • New York • London

First published in 1991 by
Madison Books
4720 Boston Way
Lanham, Maryland 20706

3 Henrietta Street
London WC2E 8LU England

Distributed by National Book Network

Library of Congress Cataloging-in-Publication Data

Dabney, Virginius, 1901-
The Jefferson scandals : a rebuttal / Virginius Dabney.
p.   cm.
Reprint. Originally published: New York :
Dodd, Mead, ©1981.
Includes bibliographical references and index.
    1. Jefferson, Thomas, 1743-1826—Relations with
women. 2. Hemings, Sally. 3. Presidents—United
States—Biography.   I. Title.
E332.2.D3   1990
973,4'5'092—dc20   [B]   90-45905 CIP

ISBN 0-8191-7863-2 (cloth)
ISBN 0-8191-7821-7 (pbk)

British Cataloging in Publication Information Available

TO
Jay, Kathy, Sally, Rob, Lucy, Bill, Taylor, Heath, Beau,
and Sarah,
my beloved grandchildren,
in the hope that they will all come to appreciate
the greatness of Thomas Jefferson.

Acknowledgments

I am especially indebted to Merrill Peterson for his kindness in giving the entire manuscript of this book a critical reading and, by virtue of his scholarly knowledge and insights, offering me valuable advice, and saving me from various errors. James A. Bear, Jr., another leading authority, also read the manuscript and rendered indispensable assistance, especially in providing important illustrations. Any errors remaining in the work are, of course, my responsibility.

I wish to express my sense of obligation to Alexander Burnham, managing editor of Dodd, Mead & Company, for suggesting that I write this book, and for his many significant contributions and his complete cooperation. In addition, I am obliged to Genia Graves of the Dodd, Mead staff for her invaluable help.

I am grateful to the accommodating staff of the Virginia State Library for many favors. Jon Kukla has placed me deeply in his debt. Toni H. Waller and Richard C. Eck were notably helpful with illustrations; and others at the library to whom I am obligated for assistance are Katherine M. Smith and Anne M. Smith. My thanks also to the always cooperative staffs of the Richmond Public Library, the Virginia Historical Society, the University of Virginia Library, the Henry E. Huntington Library, and the Reference Department of Richmond Newspapers, Inc. My appreciation goes to Stephen

H. Hochman, Alonzo T. Dill, C. Maurice Flinn, and Shearer D. Bowman for timely assistance. Joan Baxter aided me greatly by copying the manuscript in a professional manner. My wife Douglas afforded moral support, critical comment and tolerance of my demanding work schedule.

Virginius Dabney
January 1, 1981

I am greatly indebted to Madison Books for its publication of new editions of this book in both cloth and paperback.

Those in the organization to whom I am heavily indebted are Jed Lyons, Charles Lean, Gisèle Byrd, Elizabeth Wilfong, and Lynn Gemmell. Each of them has been immensely helpful at all times. I wish also to thank Alf J. Mapp, Jr. for his important role in bringing about these two editions. I also desire to express my appreciation to Pat Cecil Hass for her wonderfully intelligent and concerned assistance with the paperback edition published by Dodd, Mead in 1988.

Virginius Dabney
November 1, 1990

Contents

Illustrations

The
Jefferson
Scandals
A REBUTTAL

1

Introduction

Largely forgotten charges that Thomas Jefferson had a handsome light-skinned slave as his mistress for several decades have been resurrected in a recent Jefferson biography. This book was followed by a popular novel elaborating upon the same theme. The appearance of these works has brought to public attention allegations that were first given currency a year after Jefferson became president of the United States in 1801. Growing out of the charges were others to the effect that a beautiful daughter of the master of Monticello and his purported paramour was sold into prostitution in the New Orleans slave market, with Jefferson's knowledge and consent.

The late Fawn Brodie, author of the biography *Thomas Jefferson: An Intimate History*, and Barbara Chase-Riboud, who wrote the novel *Sally Hemings*, say categorically that Jefferson had Sally for his concubine during thirty-eight years, a relationship that resulted in five children. The claim that Jefferson fathered these children is based to a considerable degree on so-called psychological evidence and the result purports to be "psychohistory."

The question whether the allegations are true is actually a peripheral one, since the renown of Jefferson as an innovator in government, education, science, law, architecture, agriculture, and other fields is such that nothing can shake it. However, revival of the charges makes it highly desirable that they be appraised.

Brodie and Chase-Riboud have described the charges as completely authentic. Their volumes were chosen by major book clubs and reprinted in paperback editions, with large sales and widespread publicity in the printed and electronic press. Furthermore, the allegations they made have been accepted as valid by an astonishing percentage of the mass media, as well as by countless individuals. At least two national television networks have seriously considered developing miniseries based on the Chase-Riboud novel, and efforts are under way as of this writing to interest a motion picture producer. *Parade*, the huge-circulation Sunday newspaper supplement, declared flatly that Jefferson had Sally as his mistress and begat a brood of children. *The New York Times* and the *Chicago Tribune* have tended to support the charge, a substantial number of reviewers have accepted the story as true, and publications as diverse as *Newsweek*, the *Washingtonian*, and the *Unitarian World* have published categorical statements that the liaison existed.

As further evidence of the extent to which the Jefferson-Hemings allegations have permeated the national consciousness, a *New York Times* writer quoted the following from casual conversation at the American Revolution Roundtable in historic Fraunces Tavern, New York, in December 1980: "Oh juicy—I've got files . . . on whether the President of the United States can be subpoenaed to prove he seduced his slaves."

This massive acceptance by major elements of the media—and apparently of the public—occurred despite the fact that the three internationally recognized authorities on Jefferson's life and career have found the books to be wholly unsound. Historians reviewing the Brodie biography for such scholarly publications as the *Journal of American History* and the *Journal of Southern History* have also expressed supreme skepticism, if not outright disbelief, but the circulations of these academically oriented organs are minuscule in comparison to the enormous audience of the mass media and the large sales of the books in question. The Brodie biography was the bestselling hardcover historical work to appear in 1974, and there was a British edition as well. It is obvious, therefore, that the task of combating these charges is a difficult one, especially since so many persons are prone to accept accusations of this sort against important public men. But in the interests of justice and historical accuracy, it is necessary that the other side of the case be given. This is all the more essential in view of Mrs. Brodie's contention that "shame" over his relations with Sally lessened Jefferson's effectiveness as a public figure.

I, of course, make no claim to mastery of all the facts affecting the multifaceted career of Thomas Jefferson—that would be the work of decades—but I have read everything that I could find bearing upon his guilt or innocence in this matter. As a result, I have reached quite definite conclusions.

It is hardly surprising that some persons suspected Thomas Jefferson during his lifetime of fathering the mulattoes in question. The presence over the years at Monticello, Jefferson's home in Virginia, of more than a dozen almost white children could not fail to arouse suspicion. It was apparent that a white male or males were taking advantage of the slave women on the mountaintop.

In an oft-quoted passage in her *A Diary from Dixie*, written on the eve of the Civil War, Mary Boykin Chesnut of South Carolina said, "God forgive us, but ours is a monstrous system, a wrong and an iniquity! Like the patriarchs of old, our men live all in one house with their wives and their concubines; and the mulattoes one sees in every family partly resemble the white children. Any lady is ready to tell you who is the father of all the mulatto children in everybody's household but her own. Those, she seems to think, drop from the clouds."

In saying that "the mulattoes one sees in every family partly resemble the white children," Mrs. Chesnut was clearly exaggerating, since no such condition existed in anything like "every family," but the situation was bad enough. Monticello, in the late eighteenth and early nineteenth centuries, exemplified miscegenation to a lamentable degree.

The techniques of psychohistory upon which Mrs. Brodie relied were popularized by Harvard professor emeritus Erik Erikson. This type of historical writing will be judged by specific examples given in the chapters that follow. It is regarded with much skepticism by many historians.

Mrs. Brodie's approach to biography, pursuant to Erikson's theories, is not precisely that of Lytton Strachey, although it seems, when superficially examined, to be similar. E. M. Forster has written that Strachey worked from within, and thereby brought his characters psychologically alive. Forster claimed that by getting inside his subjects, Strachey was able to bring whole societies to life, and in so doing to revolutionize the art of biography. But John Halperin, a member of the University of Southern California faculty, indicates that Strachey was a good deal of a fraud. He quotes the noted biographer Leon Edel as saying of him, "One may expect that the reverse of what he says is usually the truth." Halperin asserts that "most of the time . . . he [Strachey] distorts or simply changes" the facts, and he accuses Strachey of "deliberate lies."[1] No one, of course, accuses Fawn Brodie or Erik Erikson of anything of the sort, but in her Jefferson biography Brodie stresses what she regards as psychological insights to a quite unusual degree.

As for Chase-Riboud, her novel *Sally Hemings* is an example of the type of fiction that has lately come to be known as "faction." In other words, the author and publisher claim a substantial amount of factual accuracy. Chase-Riboud does say that "my Sally Hemings is not the historical Sally Hemings," but her basic contention is that Jefferson had Sally for his mistress, and the entire book revolves about that assumption. Furthermore, the novel purports to place the principal characters in a setting that is historically accurate.

While the term "faction" is new, the writing of novels,

poems, and plays based on actual events is as old as literature itself. Innumerable examples could be mentioned—Chaucer's *Canterbury Tales,* many of Shakespeare's plays, and Scott's novels come to mind from years gone by, while more recent works such as Irving Stone's *The Agony and the Ecstasy,* Gore Vidal's *Burr,* and Herman Wouk's *The Winds of War* also exemplify the genre.

Publishers of "faction" indulge at times in extravagant claims to historical authenticity. Such, for example, was the case with Vidal's *Burr,* whose publisher declared that "the facts are actual" and "the portraits of the major characters . . . are from their own words and from the observations of their contemporaries." Yet the book gave far from a true picture, and many of the "facts" were in error or invented. Similarly, the author and publisher of *Sally Hemings* described that work as soundly researched, especially as it relates to the master of Monticello and his comely slave. We shall see to what extent that description is justified.

On its face, Mrs. Brodie's biography makes a formidable impression. There are no fewer than fifty-five pages of notes and eight pages of bibliography. As pointed out above, the author states positively that the Jefferson-Hemings relationship is a proven fact. This contrasts with the posture of the leading authorities on Jefferson, who believe strongly that all the probabilities point to the incorrectness of Brodie's charges. And they believe, furthermore, that there is a logical and plausible explanation for the paternity of Sally Hemings's children—an explanation that will be set forth in detail later in this book. These scholars recognize that Thomas Jefferson had his faults, but they are convinced that fathering Sally Hemings's brood was not one of them.

I was distressed to read in January of Mrs. Brodie's death, as I had no inkling of her illness. My book had been finished in December, and I assumed that she would perhaps wish to reply to my rebuttal.

2
How It All Began

Thomas Jefferson is one of the principal historical victims of the current orgy of debunking. He is among the Founding Fathers who we are told had feet of clay, while certain villains of the nation's early years—Benedict Arnold and Aaron Burr, for example—are now alleged to have been not so bad, after all. In the 1920s, facts were similarly stood on their heads.

The debunking of Jefferson began when a vicious, unscrupulous disappointed office-seeker named James T. Callender disseminated to the nation in 1802 the allegation that Jefferson had the slave Sally Hemings as his concubine. Had it not been for Callender, recently revived charges to the same effect probably would never have come to national attention.

Callender was a Scot who fled to the United States in the 1790s to avoid trial for sedition. A pamphleteer of undoubted gifts, with a slashing, vituperative journalistic style, Callender had attacked the British government with such unbridled vehemence that he felt it wise to put the Atlantic Ocean between himself and the authorities in London. Arriving in this country, he obtained employment on the *Philadelphia Gazette*, an organ of the Republican Party, this country's first opposition party, where his talent for invective was soon manifest, along with his penchant for stirring up trouble. His assaults on the Federalists were gratifying to Jefferson, who cooperated for a time with this controversial and obnoxious individual.

6

It should be noted that in those days political rivalries were extremely sharp, and Jefferson, for all his fine qualities and great abilities, was a political animal. Unaware at that time of Callender's utter lack of scruples, he saw in the Scot an opportunity to smite the rival Federalists. In working with Callender, Jefferson undoubtedly went too far, just as the Federalists did in accusing the Virginia aristocrat of misdeeds of which he was not even remotely guilty.

The bellicose Scotsman bounced around from one job to another, but continued his anti-Federalist blasts. In 1797 Vice-President Thomas Jefferson paid a personal call on him at his place of work in a Philadelphia printing office. Soon thereafter Callender caused a major sensation by publishing in his *History of the Year 1796*—a supplement to the anti-Federalist *American Annual Register*—charges that Alexander Hamilton, as secretary of the treasury, had put his hand in the till and taken out government funds for his personal use. It wasn't true, but Hamilton was so shaken by the charges that he felt it necessary to explain the mysterious financial dealings to which Callender referred. He said he had been blackmailed by the husband of a Mrs. Reynolds, with whom he, a married man, had had a love affair, and that he had to produce substantial sums from his personal funds to keep the matter quiet. Thus, thanks to Callender, the whole sordid story of Hamilton's adultery broke into the open, and the audacious newspaperman had scored a political ten-strike.

Jefferson was buying Callender's writings during these years, and when the latter was out of a job, the vice-president sent him $50.[1] In 1799 Callender landed a place on the Republican *Richmond Examiner*, edited by Jefferson's friend Meriwether Jones. He also began writing a tract called *The Prospect Before Us*. He carried on his crusade against the Federalists and all their works with an avalanche of his accustomed billingsgate. Jefferson was pleased with the first installment and wrote Callender, "Such papers cannot fail to produce the best effects."[2] However, the *Norfolk Herald*, as quoted in the *Richmond Examiner* of October 20, 1802, said, "It is reduced to a certainty that when Mr. Jefferson wrote his . . . letter to Callender, he had seen only two sheets on the 'Prospect,' and these two sheets are by far the least exceptionable of any in the whole work." By contrast, Fawn Brodie, in her *Thomas Jefferson: An Intimate History* (page 320), contends that the first installment included at least twenty pages.

Be that as it may, Callender was indicted and tried under the notorious Sedition Act of 1798 for defaming President Adams. The trial was held in Richmond before Justice Samuel Chase, as rabid a partisan of the Federalists as Callender was of the Republicans. The defendant got nine months in the Richmond jail and a $200 fine. He began serving his term while continuing work on *The Prospect Before Us*. He also corresponded with Jefferson from Richmond's none too salubrious bastille, which he termed "this den of wretchedness and horror."

When Jefferson became president in 1801, he pardoned all who had been convicted under the sedition law, including Callender. He directed that Callender be released from jail and promised remission of his fine. There were unanticipated delays in refunding the money, and the president finally paid part of it from his own pocket. Callender was infuriated by the government's failure to remit promptly and was not mollified by Jefferson's payment of a portion. He brooded over his maltreatment and was determined to seek the Richmond postmastership, which paid $1,500 a year, as a reward for his services to the Republican Party. However, correspondence with Secretary of State James Madison and a visit to Washington, D.C., failed to produce the appointment. President Jefferson did not respond to his communications.

Callender began thereupon to make threatening noises. If Jefferson was unwilling to reward him with the postmastership, he would release information damaging to the president.

The latter was undisturbed and declared that Callender was after "hush money"—a phrase believed by many to be of more modern origin. "He knows nothing of me which I am not willing to declare before the world," Jefferson wrote Governor James Monroe of Virginia. He added that his financial and other assistance to Callender had been offered in the form of charity to "a man of genius suffering from persecution, and not as a writer in our politics." This was hardly in accord with the facts, and Monroe told his friend that he would be wise to drop the unconvincing claim that his motives were purely charitable in nature. He also urged Jefferson to get from Callender "all letters, however unimportant."[3]

Callender lost little time in carrying out his threats. He returned to Richmond and obtained employment on the *Recorder*, a Federalist weekly, the precise type of publication with which he had been in total disagreement a short time before. Ensconced there, he began assaulting President Jefferson savagely.

A highly embellished and distorted version of "the Walker affair," something that had occurred a third of a century before, in 1768, when Jefferson was unmarried, was one of his opening salvos. John Walker had gone to New York State for four months, leaving his wife and baby in care of his friend Jefferson. The latter made some sort of attempt at making love to Betsey Walker in her husband's absence and was rebuffed. Callender leaped upon this long-forgotten episode and depicted the master of Monticello as a lecherous beast and base betrayer of his friend's trust. The episode, embellished with Callender's gross exaggerations, was used later in political campaigns by Jefferson's enemies. Walker himself in subsequent years depicted Jefferson as pursuing his wife over a period of more than a decade, waiting outside her bedroom in his shirttails to seize her. She was said to have repulsed him on one occasion with a pair of scissors. Tom Paine remarked somewhat skeptically, "We have heard of the siege of Troy, but whoever heard of a ten-year siege to seduce?"

There is no reason to believe that anything but the relatively mild episode of 1768 ever occurred. As was his wont, Jefferson made no public denial, but he did write Robert Smith, secretary of the navy in his cabinet, in 1805, "You will perceive that I plead guilty to one of their charges, that when young and single I offered love to a handsome lady. I acknowledge its incorrectness. It is the only one founded on truth among all their allegations against me."[4]

Explaining his unwillingness to enter into public denials of the numerous charges being bandied about then and later, Jefferson wrote to Samuel Smith in 1798: "Were I to undertake to answer the calumnies of the newspapers, it would be more than all my own time, and that of twenty aids could effect, for while I should be answering one, twenty new ones would be invented. I have thought it better to trust to the justice of my countrymen that they would judge me by what they see of my conduct on the stage where they have placed me."

Callender's highly colored version of *l'affaire* Walker was bad enough, but his lurid allegations concerning Jefferson's relations with Sally Hemings, a handsome and almost white Monticello slave, were even worse.

Rumors had been floating around Charlottesville that Jefferson had fathered a mulatto brood on his mountaintop, but until Callender got wind of them they had not traveled far. When the feisty Scotsman put his superb talents for vilification to work on the case, his vivid accounts in the *Richmond Recorder* of Jefferson's "Congo harem" and "black Venus" were gleefully republished throughout the country in the Federalist press.

Callender never bothered to verify the rumors that he picked up in the purlieus of Charlottesville concerning Jefferson and Sally Hemings, nor did any other newspaper send a reporter to Monticello to check on their authenticity.[5] With no libel laws in that era worthy of the name, Callender could give his imagination free rein, and his allegations concerning "Dusky Sally" and "Black Sal" were broadcast to the world. Jefferson was depicted as capering with "the black wench and her mulatto litter," and his long vacations at Monticello while president were, of course, due to his insatiable lust for the "mahogany colored charmer."

Callender was not content to assail Jefferson for his supposed relations with Sally Hemings and his role in the Walker affair. He also charged him with paying off a private debt in depreciated money.

Jefferson was quite naturally enraged by these ferocious attacks on his character from a man who had previously praised him unstintingly. But, as noted, his only denials were made privately. "Every decent man among them [the Federalists] revolts at his [Callender's] filth," he wrote to Robert Livingston. It was an overoptimistic appraisal; most Federalists, decent or no, were only too happy to revel in any denunciations of their archrival.

The president of the United States must have been even more distraught when ribald verses celebrating his purported liaison with Sally began appearing in the hostile press. There was, for example, the series of verses in the *Boston Gazette*, republished in the *Philadelphia Port Folio*. The lengthy versification is too long for complete quotation, but it opened with the following:

> Of all the damsels on the green
> On mountain or in valley
> A lass so luscious ne'er was seen
> As Monticellian Sally.

And the chorus went on:

> Yankee Doodle, whose the noodle?
> What wife were half so handy?
> To breed a flock of slaves to stock
> A blackamoors the dandy.

This ebullition was followed by numerous others. Thomas Moore, the Irish poet, visited this country and found much to dislike. He returned to Great Britain and composed the following:

> The weary statesman for repose hath fled
>   From halls of council to his negro's shed
> Where blest he woos some black Aspasia's grace
>   And dreams of freedom in his slave's embrace!

Moore explained in a footnote that "the 'black Aspasia' of the present P******** of the United States . . . has given rise to much pleasantry among the anti-democratic wits of America." It should be said that the poet apologized some years later for the foregoing.[6]

Other bards of much less talent came forward. There was, for example, this in the *Philadelphia Port Folio:*

> Den Quashee [a Negro] de white wife will hab
> And Massa *Jefferson will hab de black.*

Thirteen-year-old William Cullen Bryant, in an outburst that he was said to have regretted later, addressed the chief executive of the nation as follows:

Go, wretch, resign the presidential chair,
Disclose thy secret features foul or fair . . .
Go scan, Philosophist, thy ****** charms,
And sink supinely in her sable arms;
But quit to abler hands the helm of state,
Nor image ruin on thy country's fate!

Finally, to quote one more of these effusions, the following appeared in the *Port Folio:*

Resume thy shells and butterflies,
Thy beetle's heads and lizard's thighs,
The state no more controul:
Thy tricks, with Sooty *Sal* give o'er:
Indulge thy body, Tom, no more;
But try to save thy *soul.*

Most of these verses appeared after Callender had passed to his reward. A morose and ill-tempered individual who resorted all too often to strong drink, he seemed unable to get along with anybody. His savage attacks on Jefferson increased the *Richmond Recorder*'s circulation greatly, and his name was placed on the masthead, along with that of Henry Pace. But he was soon squabbling with Pace and claiming that Pace owed him money. One July day in 1803, Callender's moody perversity led him again to the bottle. His body was found shortly thereafter in the James River, in three feet of water, and the official verdict was that he had drowned accidentally when drunk. It seems entirely possible, however, that his death was not accidental. The *Richmond Examiner* said following his demise: "Callender had threatened to put an end to his existence, by drowning himself, for several weeks previous to his actual death. . . . It may be inferred that he got excessively drunk for the express purpose of putting an easy end to his life."[7] Callender was buried in the St. John's churchyard on

Logotype of The Recorder, *the journal in which James T. Callender launched his attack on Jefferson in 1802, with allegations involving Sally Hemings. The president had just refused to appoint Callender postmaster of Richmond.*

the evening of the day he died, apparently without a marker on his grave.

James Truslow Adams, the eminent historian, wrote that "almost every scandalous story about Jefferson which is still whispered or believed" may be traced to the scurrilous writings of Callender.[8] Others, including Merrill Peterson, hold the same opinion. It is obvious, therefore, that the name of James Thomson Callender is not without significance in the early history of the United States. It is, however, highly unfortunate that his great abilities as a journalist were not directed into more constructive channels.

A succession of writers about nineteenth-century America and slavery have apparently taken their cues from Callender's defamatory diatribes. The antidemocratic Englishwoman, Mrs. Frances Trollope, in her book *Domestic Manners of the Americans*, published in 1832 following her visit to this country, wrote that Jefferson was commonly said "to have been the father of children by almost all his numerous gang of female slaves." She added that "the hospitable orgies for which Monticello was so celebrated were incomplete unless the goblets he [Jefferson] quaffed were tendered by the trembling hands of his own slave offspring." Mrs. Trollope repeated a story then circulating that Jefferson forced Sally's daughter Harriet into a life of prostitution.

Captain Frederick Marryat, another English writer, traveling through the South in 1838, reported that he had uncovered a "well-known fact, that a considerable portion of Mr. Jefferson's slaves were his own children," and that he "permitted these, his slaves and his children, the issue of his own loins, to be sold at auction after his demise, not even emancipating them, as he might have done, before his death."

A Dr. Levi Gaylord of Sodus, New York, wrote a letter in 1838 to William Goodell's weekly, *The Friend of Man*, published in Utica, New York, saying that Otis Reynolds, "a gentleman from St. Louis, Missouri, himself a practical, as well as theoretical supporter of slavery," stated that he had

witnessed the sale of Jefferson's daughter in New Orleans for
$1,000. How Reynolds knew whose daughter was being sold
is not explained. Gaylord's letter was republished a few
months later (September 21, 1838) in *The Liberator* of Boston,
William Lloyd Garrison's famous abolitionist journal. William
Wells Brown, a former slave and "the first black American to
publish a novel, a drama and a travel book," wrote a poem
entitled "Jefferson's Daughter" which was included in
Brown's songbook, *The Anti-Slavery Harp* (1848). The poem
had appeared overseas shortly before in *Tait's Edinburgh
Magazine*, preceded by the following from the *London Morning
Chronicle:* "It is asserted, on the authority of an American
newspaper, that the daughter of Thomas Jefferson, late president of the United States, was sold in New Orleans for
$1,000." This material had also been printed in *The Liberator*
(May 26, 1848). An extract from Brown's poem follows:

JEFFERSON'S DAUGHTER

Can the blood that at Lexington poured o'er the plain,
    When the sons warred with tyrants their rights to
       uphold,
Can the tide of Niagara wipe out the stain?
    No! Jefferson's child has been bartered for gold!

The daughter of Jefferson sold for a slave!
    The child of a freeman for dollars and francs!
The roar of applause, when your orators rave,
    Is lost in the sound of her chain, as it clanks . . .

When the incense that glows before Liberty's shrine,
    Is unmixed with the blood of the galled and
       oppressed,—
O, then, and then only, the boast may be thine,
    That the stripes and stars wave o'er the land of the
       blest.

All of which inspired William Wells Brown, author of the foregoing, to write a novel entitled *Clotel, or the President's Daughter, A Narrative of Slave Life in the United States* (London, 1853).

W. Edward Farrison, emeritus professor of English at North Carolina Central University and the foremost authority on Brown's career, writes: "Brown never claimed personal acquaintance with any slave children of Jefferson. . . . Without worrying, then, whether the reports concerning Jefferson were literally true in every detail, he used them for their sensational value . . . not to attack the character of Thomas Jefferson *per se*, but to win by means of an entrancing story attention to a comprehensive and persuasive argument against American slavery."[9]

Reports of Jefferson's slave offspring were accepted as authentic by Richard Hildreth in his *History of the United States of America from the Adoption of the Federal Constitution to the End of the Sixteenth Congress* (New York, 1856). He charged that the master of Monticello had a "semi-African concubine," said to have been his wife's half-sister, who bore him several children. Hildreth asserted that these allegations had not been authoritatively contradicted.

In 1860 a newspaper hostile to Abraham Lincoln, the *Chicago Times and Herald*, published a speech supposedly made by Lincoln in his campaign for the presidency in which he denounced Jefferson as a hypocrite "continually puling about liberty and equality," but who "brought his own children to the hammer, and made money of his debaucheries." Lincoln branded the article at once "a bold and deliberate forgery."

The *Illinois State Journal* (September 6, 1860), in a comment which the editor of the *Collected Works of Abraham Lincoln* said "may have been written by Lincoln and was certainly authorized by him," declared, "Mr. Lincoln never used any such language in any speech *at any time*. Throughout the whole of his political life, Mr. Lincoln has ever spoken of Mr. Jefferson in the most kindly and respectful manner, holding him up as one of the ablest statesmen of his own or any other age. . . . This is so well known that any attempt, by means of fraud and forgery, to create a contrary opinion, can only react upon the desperate politicians who are parties to such disreputable tactics."[10]

By 1864 the novel *Clotel* by William Wells Brown, which had been published more than a decade before in London, appeared in Boston in a new guise. The name had been changed to *Clotelle: A Tale of the Southern States*, and Thomas Jefferson had disappeared from its pages. The slave girl reputedly sold in New Orleans had been metamorphosed into the daughter of a senator.[11] The novel was still deemed useful propaganda for the abolitionist cause.

Frederick Douglass, the former slave and noted Negro leader, joined those who contended that Jefferson had fathered a brood of mulattoes. Merrill Peterson points out that Douglass added a new twist to the story by saying that one of Jefferson's granddaughters was among the free Negroes who had emigrated to Liberia.

During the Reconstruction era, material concerning Jefferson's purported illegitimate descendants was used as evidence of the odious aspects of slavery. Then for about three-quarters of a century after the Civil War little was heard concerning the charges broadcast back in 1802 by Callender. But in 1954 *Ebony* magazine, published by blacks, revived the legend by producing a prominent display of Negroes who claimed to be descended from the squire of Monticello.

In 1956 J. C. Furnas issued his *Goodbye to Uncle Tom*, a Book-of-the-Month Club selection, wherein he said flatly, "Jefferson was only one of many eminent and sometimes aristocratic slaveowners who left mulatto offspring." Furnas conceded that some Jefferson scholars disagreed, but he accepted the story, and reviewers of his book spread the allegations.

In another Book-of-the-Month Club selection, *Image of America* (1959), Father R. L. Bruckberger, a Dominican priest, repeatedly expressed the highest admiration for Jefferson in most respects, but he saw no reason to doubt that *two* of Jefferson's daughters "by an octoroon female slave were . . . taken to New Orleans after Jefferson's death, and sold in the slave market at $1,000 each to be used for unmentionable purposes. . . . The youngest daughter escaped from her master and committed suicide by drowning herself to escape the horrors of her position" (pages 66–67). Bruckberger excerpted the foregoing from a statement of Alexander Ross, a Canadian who, he said, "held responsible posts in his own country and was moreover a personal friend of Abraham Lincoln." It is unfortunate that Ross failed to ask his friend Lincoln about the story, since the Great Emancipator would doubtless have enlightened him. It is also unfortunate that Bruckberger did not make a thorough inquiry before giving credence to this sensational canard.

In his *Ordeal of Ambition* (1970), Jonathan Daniels rejected the charge involving the New Orleans slave market, but he propelled the allegation concerning a liaison between Jefferson and Sally further into the public arena. His book deals primarily with the careers of Jefferson, Hamilton, and Burr, and contains only incidental references to the supposed relations between the author of the Declaration of Independence and his slave. Daniels said this charge could not be proved one way or the other, but he believed the relationship may well have existed.

The various allegations as to Harriet's "sale" would seem to have been completely refuted by her brother Madison in an interview he gave to the *Pike County* (Ohio) *Republican* in 1873. At that time he said, "Harriet married a white man in good standing in Washington City, whose name I could give, but will not, for prudential reasons. She raised a family of children. . . . I have not heard from her for ten years, and do

not know whether she is dead or alive."[12] Not a word from
Madison Hemings about any sale in New Orleans—or from
several other relatives of Harriet who were interviewed at
various times. Pearl N. Graham, writing in the *Journal of Negro
History* in 1961 declared, "Four descendants of Harriet Hemings said Harriet had been married in Canada," which Ms.
Graham described as "a section of Charlottesville." "We are
now agreed," she went on, "that Harriet Hemings spent her
lifetime in or near Albemarle County, Virginia."[13] One may
take his choice between these two conflicting versions. That of
Madison Hemings appears the more specific and convincing.
The thing that seems certain is that Mrs. Trollope, Captain
Marryat, Dr. Gaylord, the mysterious Otis Reynolds who
"saw" Jefferson's daughter sold, William Lloyd Garrison's
Liberator, William Wells Brown and his *Clotel, Tait's Edinburgh
Magazine*, the *London Morning Chronicle*, Frederick Douglass,
the *Chicago Times and Herald*, Alexander Ross, and Father R.
L. Bruckberger, to mention no others, all went off half-cocked
in repeating this fantastic slander against Thomas Jefferson.
As for the second "daughter" who drowned herself rather than
enter a life of shame, the idea of this is too absurd for further
discussion.

     The references to the supposed sale in New Orleans and
to reported amours at Monticello in the recent Furnas and
Bruckberger books were incidental to those volumes' main
themes. Bruckberger presented a broad picture of the United
States, with only about one page devoted to the alleged
auction. Furnas addressed himself to the race situation as a
whole, with only passing allusion to purported happenings on
Jefferson's mountaintop.

     Then in 1974 Professor Fawn Brodie of the University of
California at Los Angeles produced a biography of Jefferson
revolving to a predominant degree around his reputed relationship with Sally Hemings. There was no acceptance in
this "psycho-historical study" of stories that Jefferson's al-

In a recent conversation with Mr. Otis Reynolds, a gentleman from St. Louis, Missouri, himself a practical, as well as theoretical supporter of slavery in our discussion on the subject, Mr. Reynolds endeavored to find an apology for the "domestic institutions" of the South, by assuming, as a fact, the alleged inferiority of the colored race.

I replied, that it was currently reported here, that the "best blood of Virginia, flowed in the veins of the slaves," and the argument could, therefore, be of no force, in regard to the amalgamated portion of the slaves. Said he, with much emphasis,

☞ "That's true; I saw myself, the DAUGHTER of THOMAS JEFFERSON sold in New Orleans, for ONE THOUSAND DOLLARS." ☜

What a fact for the contemplation of this free republic!! and what a comment on our professions of love for liberty, and practice of slavery!!!

☞ *The daughter of the President of the United States, the boasted land of freedom, sold into interminable bondage!!!* ☜ Look at it, citizens of our free republic! Here is no violation of law—you have the natural, legalized working of the system

COURTESY OF THE VIRGINIA STATE LIBRARY

The abolitionist press in 1838 carried the above spurious claim by a man who said he saw Jefferson's daughter sold into slavery in New Orleans. This was completely disproved.

legedly illegitimate children were sold in New Orleans slave
markets, and Brodie pronounced these stories "dubious," but
there was a great deal concerning his "paternity" of various
Hemingses. Mrs. Brodie presented no important new factual
material in behalf of her thesis, but she subjected Jefferson's
personality and career to her own novel interpretations. The
result was a book that was in direct conflict with the views of
Dumas Malone, Merrill Peterson, and the late Julian Boyd.
Henry S. Randall, whose exhaustive three-volume life of
Jefferson appeared in 1857, did not mention the charges in
that work, but was convinced of Jefferson's personal morality.
Mrs. Brodie's book was well written, contained extensive
notes and bibliography, and was evidently based on considerable research. Only careful and thorough students of Jefferson's career were able to pinpoint its weaknesses. Brodie was
not a specialist on Jefferson; she had written three previous
biographies of individuals having no relation to Jefferson or his
period.

Mrs. Brodie's *Thomas Jefferson: An Intimate History*, with
its startling charges, was a Book-of-the-Month Club selection
and a great commercial success. The public dotes on exposés
of purported philanderings of the great. The paperback edition bore on the back cover the words "The Sensual Jefferson." A number of reviewers praised the work highly, but no
recognized authority on Jefferson did so. On the contrary,
several of these scholars were caustic in their criticism.

In the pages that follow we shall examine the contents of
the Brodie biography in detail.

3

The Hemingses of Monticello

The Hemings family at Monticello included several slaves who demonstrated unusual abilities. Sally Hemings, about whom the still-reverberating controversy revolves, could have been among the least talented, although she may have been the handsomest. The slave Isaac Jefferson, in his 1847 reminiscences, termed her "mighty near white . . . very handsome: long straight hair down her back." Thomas Jefferson Randolph, Jefferson's grandson, described her as "light colored and decidedly good looking."

There is little authoritative information concerning Sally's talents. As a fourteen-year-old girl accompanying Polly Jefferson to Paris, where Jefferson went as emissary (stopping off in London), she did not impress Abigail Adams, wife of John Adams, the future president of the United States. Abigail wrote that "the girl [Sally] . . . is quite a child, and Captain Ramsey is of opinion will be of so little Service that he had better carry her back with him."[1] This hardly seems a fair judgment, in view of Sally's extreme youth and quite understandable unease in a totally strange environment. Once Sally got to Paris with Polly and was tutored in French, she appears to have carried out her duties as maid and companion satisfactorily.

Roll of the negroes according to their ages.
Albemarle.

1737	1793	1811

1737 Squire 8 mar. 23. died 5. 1810.
31. ...... 8 May 5. 1810.
'43 ......
.... 8 Sep. 1810
.... 1810
.... 8 Apr. 21. 1811

'53. John
'55. Davy
'56. Quarry
'57. Bell
.... 8. 189.
'59 Betty Brown
'60 Ned
.... Lewis
'61 Nance
'62. Jenny Pied's
'63 Isaac
....
'69 Critta
'70 Peter Hemings
....
73. Sally
.... 75. John Hemings
.... 76. James
.... 8.

1793. Edward
.... Virginia Bagg's
.... 9a Scilla Ned's
.... Dolly Birtle's
.... Jonathan
.... James Lewis
.... Esther
'96 Philip
......
.... Gawen Ned's
.... Ursula Jenny's
'97. Sanco
.... Ambrose
.... Eston
.... Ben
....
'98 Gilbert, ...
.... Ned's
....
.... Fanny Page's
.... Isabel Lewis's
.... Thrimston Ned's
.... Israel Ned's
.... Louisa Jenny's
.01 Critta Ann Nance's?
.... Peg Bet's
....

1811 Apr. 1 Lewis Ursula's
Sep. Jenny Scilla's
Dec. Jenny Fanny's
Oct. Matilda Ursula's
Dec. 20. Robert Virginia's
1812. Oct. 27. Zachariah Nance's
Dec. 6 Betsey Ann Edy's
1813. Fanny Lucinda Esther's
Nov. Edmund Richard's?
.... Fanny Scilla's & Mar. 1816 Johnny's
.... Mary Lucinda & Mar. 1816 comp.
Oct. 1. Thomas Ursula's
1814. May Marshal Mary's [.. a Lucinda's]
....
June ....
1815. Jan. 5. Peter Edy's
July James David Critta's
Aug. Patsy Mose's
Sep. Amanda Virginia's
1816. Jan. 31 Louisa Ursula's
April 15 Betsy Maria's
July ....
....

COURTESY OF THE MASSACHUSETTS HISTORICAL SOCIETY

Jefferson's Farm Book (page 30), with birth dates for Monticello slaves. Sally (Hemings) is shown to have been born in 1773.

Upon her return to Monticello some two years later with Jefferson and his daughters, she was listed in Jefferson's highly detailed *Farm Book* as a house servant and apparently was a seamstress. She is noted there to have received food, clothing, and blankets along with the other house servants. While her precise place of residence at Monticello is not known, "it is certain that she was not housed in the main house," says James A. Bear, Jr., resident director at Monticello.[2] This important statement comes from the best-informed person concerning the rooms at Monticello, their history, and who lived in them and when. Those who speak of a "secret room" for Sally adjoining Jefferson's, or a staircase by which she was alleged to have descended to his bedroom from a room above, should note Bear's authoritative denial. (See Chapter 5 for further information concerning the staircase.)

There seem to be no anecdotes concerning Sally. Neither is she mentioned even once in all the known correspondence between Jefferson and his daughters. Callender's slanders and those which followed, together with the reminiscences of three elderly former slaves at Monticello recorded long after Jefferson's death, constitute the basis for the legends that have been spread far and wide.

Sally and the other Hemingses at Monticello apparently were descendants of John Wayles, a native-born Englishman who came to Virginia, and Elizabeth or Betty Hemings, a "bright mulatto" who was his slave. Betty was the daughter of Captain Hemings, an English seafaring man who stopped off in Virginia, and a "full-blooded African" woman, Madison Hemings said in his *Pike County Republican* interview. Whether this is correct is uncertain. In any event, Jefferson's *Farm Book* says Betty was born about 1735. Apparently her mother was a slave on the plantation of Francis Eppes IV at Bermuda Hundred. In 1746 Betty was deeded to John Wayles as part of his marriage dowry when he wed Martha Eppes. Wayles took her as his concubine in 1761 after the death of his third wife, according to common report. Isaac Jefferson, the former Monticello slave, declared in 1847, "Folks said that these Hemingses was old Mr. Wayles' children." Madison Hemings confirmed this in 1873, and it apparently was true. The six children, in order of birth, were Robert, James, Thenia, Critta, Peter, and Sally, the youngest, who was born in 1773.

John Wayles, be it noted, was not only the reputed father of these children; he was also the father of Mrs. Thomas Jefferson, née Martha Wayles, John Wayles's daughter by his first wife, Martha Eppes. Hence Sally Hemings and her brothers and sisters were seemingly the half-brothers and sisters of Martha Jefferson. It is doubtful whether Mrs. Jefferson knew that her father supposedly sired these individuals, but Thomas Jefferson almost certainly did know. This would seem to explain why the Hemingses were given preferred positions at Monticello. All were house servants, and none was required to labor in the fields.

After the death of John Wayles in 1773, Betty Hemings had two additional children. The father of her son John was Joseph Neilson, a white carpenter working at Monticello. John Hemings became a highly talented cabinetmaker. Betty had had four children by one or more black fathers before her liaison with Wayles. One of them, Mary, was the mother of Joe Fosset, who also became a craftsman at Monticello. Another, Bett or Betty Brown, was the future mother of Wormeley, Monticello's chief slave gardener, and Burwell, Jefferson's last personal servant, to whom he was deeply devoted. (In attempting to unravel the tangled genealogies of the various generations of Hemingses and to relate their accomplishments, I have relied on the thorough and informative article by James A. Bear, Jr., on the Hemings family in the autumn 1979 issue of *Virginia Cavalcade*.)

We come now to the famous Sally Hemings and her children, one of whom, Harriet, died in infancy. There is a ref-

erence in the *Farm Book* (p. 50) to "Sally Edy 2" under the
"Bread-list for 1796," which is interpreted by Mrs. Brodie to
mean that there was a child of Sally's named Edy. But Edy is
mentioned on page 130, under the date 1787, which means
that she was born in that year, when Sally was only 14 and
either en route to or just arrived in Paris. Obviously she was
not Sally's child. Four of Sally's children—Harriet (the
second of that name), Beverly, Madison, and Eston—sur-
vived. It was this second Harriet, a beautiful woman according to all accounts, who was the subject of the widely
published and completely untrue report that she had been sold
into prostitution in the New Orleans slave market. She and
Beverly ran away from Monticello in 1822, and Jefferson
made no effort to bring them back. Harriet married and lived
either in Albemarle County or Washington, D.C. Madison
and Eston were freed under Jefferson's will. They moved to
Ohio in the mid-1830s, and Eston subsequently went to
Wisconsin. Both died in the middle west.

As for Sally herself, she was still a slave at Monticello
when Jefferson died in 1826. There is no record of exactly
when she left, but presumably she was freed by Martha
Jefferson Randolph. Madison Hemings stated in his 1873
interview that he and Eston "rented a house and took mother
to live with us," after she was freed. He added that Sally died
in 1835. It was then that he and Eston moved to Ohio.

Several male Hemingses of the third generation at
Monticello, brothers of Sally, were given a large degree of
freedom in moving about. They were not only intelligent, but
were educated well beyond the general run of slaves.

Robert, the eldest, a "bright mulatto," traveled with
Jefferson on trips to Philadelphia, Annapolis, and elsewhere.
During the sojourn in Annapolis he took a two months' course
in barbering under a well-known tonsorial expert. "Few, if
any, restrictions were ever placed on Robert," James Bear
writes.

*Deed of manumission freeing Robert Hemings, dated December 24, 1794,
signed by Thomas Jefferson and his nephew Dabney Carr.*

Robert married a slave woman named Dolly whom he met on a trip to Fredericksburg. She remained there, but her husband was at Monticello most of the time when he was not traveling around. Jefferson often had trouble locating him.

This slave was manumitted in 1794 under unusual circumstances. Dr. George Frederick Stras of Fredericksburg was the owner of Dolly, Robert's wife. Robert was quite naturally anxious to be reunited with her and their baby, so Stras initiated manumission proceedings and agreed to pay Jefferson for him. Jefferson was not at all happy over relinquishing Robert, and the latter was disturbed over being separated from his master. Jefferson told his son-in-law, Thomas Mann Randolph, Jr., that Stras "debauched him from me." Martha Randolph wrote her father that Robert had "expressed great uneasiness at having quitted you in the manner he did. . . . The poor creature seems so deeply impressed with a sense of ingratitude as to be rendered quite unhappy by it, but he could not prevail upon himself to give up his wife and child."

The Robert Hemingses moved to Richmond after he was freed and apparently worked for Stras temporarily. Then Robert went into business for himself. His name appears in the 1799 city personal property list as the owner of two horses or mules on which he paid a tax of twenty-four cents. Three years later he lived on a half-acre lot that he owned at today's Seventh and Grace, then Seventh and G Streets, where evidently he operated a livery stable or freight-hauling agency. He and Jefferson apparently became reconciled in later years, since Robert did some errands for him. The accidental discharge of a pistol caused Robert to lose a hand, we learn from Isaac Jefferson. Robert died in Richmond in 1819.[3]

James Hemings, Sally's older brother who went to Paris with Jefferson, was exceptionally intelligent. He was house servant, messenger, and driver during the years when his master was governor of Virginia. He served as guide to a traveling Englishman in Richmond. Then in 1784 Jefferson said he would take James to Paris with him "for a particular purpose," which was to be trained as a *chef de cuisine* under the tutelage of the best French chefs. James learned the culinary art sufficiently well to become chef at Jefferson's Paris residence. When he and his master returned to Virginia, James became chef at Monticello.

Later, when Jefferson went to New York as secretary of state under President George Washington, James accompanied him. James also was part of the entourage in Philadelphia when the capital was moved there, and was in charge of the kitchen. Then when Jefferson retired temporarily from public life, he made a deal with James that if he taught "such a person as I shall place under him for the purpose to be a good cook," James would be freed. The slave agreed and carried out his part of the bargain; the deed of manumission was signed in 1796. His successor in the culinary department at Monticello was apparently his younger brother Peter, whom Jefferson described as a "servant of great intelligence and diligence."[4]

There were reports that freedom was too much for James, and that he began drinking heavily. Jefferson mentioned that he saw him in Philadelphia in 1797 and was relieved to find that "he is not given up to drink, as I had been informed." And Jefferson added, "He tells me his next trip will be to Spain. I am afraid his journeys will end in the moon. I have endeavored to persuade him to stay where he is, and lay up money." The trip to Spain did not take place, and James returned briefly to Monticello in 1801. He remained for only a month and a half. A few months later he committed suicide. Despite his intelligence, he appears to have been an unstable character; his suicide was ascribed to excessive drinking.[5]

The other Hemings who deserves special mention is John, Sally's half-brother, a son of Joseph Neilson and Betty Hemings. Under the tutelage of Davy Watson, a deserter from the British army, John became an expert craftsman who, according to Edmund Bacon, the overseer, "could make anything that was wanted in woodwork." He made "most of the woodwork of Mr. Jefferson's fine carriage," Bacon said.

It was reported, without absolute proof, that John Hemings made a substantial portion of the plantation furniture at Monticello, but no single piece survives that can be definitely ascribed to him. He undoubtedly made what was termed a "beautiful writing desk" for Ellen Randolph Coolidge, Jefferson's granddaughter, but it was lost at sea in 1825 with the brig *Washington*, when en route to Boston. The loss was crushing to Hemings. "Virgil could not have been more afflicted had his Aeneid fallen a prey to the flames," Jefferson wrote. He asked John if he could make another desk like it, but the craftsman replied that bad eyesight and his imperfect recollection of the piece made it impossible. When Martha Randolph was leaving Monticello in 1829, she wrote, "We shall carry . . . other articles . . . including the stained bedstead made by John Hemings neater than you would suppose, low posts with head and foot boards." John and his apprentices put a new roof on Monticello, and when Poplar Forest, Jefferson's residence in Bedford County, was damaged by fire in 1825, Jefferson wrote Francis Eppes VII, who was living there, that he would send him John Hemings and his two apprentices, Madison and Eston Hemings. John Hemings "can repair every thing of wood as well as or perhaps better than any body there," he declared.

Known to the Jefferson grandchildren and great-grandchildren as "Daddy," John was a great favorite with them, as well as with Jefferson himself, who sometimes called him "Johnny." The children enjoyed visiting "Daddy" in the carpenter's shops, where they begged him to fashion little boxes, tables, or what-not for them. He did so when he could find time from his other responsibilities.

John had a wife, but her name is not known, nor is it known if they had any children. No details are vouchsafed in the *Farm Book*. He served the Jeffersons and the Randolphs for more than half a century. John was still a slave when Jefferson died, but his master granted him freedom through a codicil in his will, along with other members of the Hemings clan. Burwell, son of Bett Hemings and in service as Jefferson's personal valet for many years, was the first to be listed in the codicil, which granted him his freedom and $300. The remainder of the codicil reads as follows:

> I give also to my good servants John Hemings and Joe Fosset [son of Mary Hemings] their freedom at the end of one year after my death, and to each of them respectively all the tools of their respective shops or callings: it is my will that a comfortable log house be built for each . . . so emancipated on some part of my lands convenient to them with respect to the residence of their wives and to Charlottesville and the University, where they be mostly employed. . . . I also give to John Hemings the service of two apprentices, Madison and Eston Hemings, until their respective ages of twenty-one years, at which period respectively I give them their freedom.[6]

Why was not Sally also freed in Jefferson's will? Mrs. Brodie, referring to Jefferson's "celebrated concubine," thinks it was because he feared her emancipation would result in unfavorable publicity and would tend to confirm the reports of his relations with her.[7] Those who do not believe that Sally was ever Jefferson's concubine agree that he might nevertheless have been reluctant to free her, since the possible notoriety might have caused the public to put credence in the canard. Hence he relied on his daughter, Martha Randolph, to free her after his death.

Thus ends the brief chronicle of the Hemings family at Monticello. Had it not been for James T. Callender's excursions into the realm of fiction, we should probably have never heard of any of them.

4

Callender, Cosway, and Sally

"A record of extraordinary concealment" is the phrase used by Brodie in her *Thomas Jefferson: An Intimate History* (page 23) to describe Jefferson's relations with Sally Hemings. If the relations that she alleges actually existed, the description is fully justified.

"A serious passion that brought Jefferson and the slave woman much private happiness over a period lasting thirty-eight years," Brodie continues (page 32). "It also brought suffering, shame and even political paralysis in regard to Jefferson's agitation for emancipation."

Callender, the original source of these charges, is termed "a generally accurate reporter" by Brodie.[1] Just what this remarkable statement is based on remains a mystery. John C. Miller, the Stanford University historian, describes Callender as "the most unscrupulous scandalmonger of the day . . . a journalist who stopped at nothing and stooped to anything. . . . Callender was not an investigative journalist; he never bothered to investigate anything . . . truth, if it stood in his way, was summarily mowed down."[2]

This wildly irresponsible pamphleteer disseminated pages of falsehoods concerning, first, such Federalists as George Washington and John Adams, and then, reversing his allegiance, such Republicans as Thomas Jefferson and James Madison. In Callender's words, Washington was "a scandalous hypocrite" who "authorized the robbery and ruin of his own army" in the Revolution for his own private gain, while Adams was "a British spy" and "one of the most egregious fools upon the continent." Of Madison Callender wrote that he "must have known all about Sally, and when he assisted in passing off the president [Jefferson] as a prodigy of virtue, he differed from the president himself precisely as much as the man that circulates a copper dollar differs from the man that forged it."

No one, not even Callender, contended that Jefferson maintained a liaison with any slave woman until well after his wife's death in 1782. He and Martha Wayles Skelton had been married for a decade when she died, not long after the birth of their sixth child. (Only two of the children grew to maturity.) Jefferson's devotion to her was profound, and slaves present around her deathbed reported—although this was never proved—that the grief-stricken husband promised her not to marry again. When Martha died, at age thirty-three, Jefferson fainted and kept to his room for three weeks.[3]

He was thirty-nine at the time of his beloved wife's passing. A few weeks before, he had declined reelection to the Virginia legislature, saying that he wished to retire from public life. The squire of Monticello had served for thirteen years in one capacity or another, including governor of Virginia and member of the Continental Congress, in which latter capacity he had penned the Declaration of Independence. His decision to withdraw from public office did not turn out to be irrevocable, for he was persuaded to serve again in the Continental Congress. There, in 1784, he presented a measure that would have prevented the spread of slavery into any territory beyond the boundaries of the original thirteen states. It was defeated by a single vote, and, as he wrote later, "heaven was silent in that awful moment." Adoption of this epochal mea-

Martha Jefferson.

Silhouette of Martha Jefferson, only known likeness of Jefferson's wife, artist unknown.

Know all men by these presents that we Thomas Jefferson and Francis Eppes are held and firmly bound to our sovereign lord the king his heirs and successors in the sum of fifty pounds current money of Virginia, to the paiment of which well and truly to be made we bind ourselves jointly and severally, our joint and several heirs executors and administrators in witness whereof we have hereto set our hands and seals this twenty third day of December in the year of our lord one thousand seven hundred and seventy one The condition of the above obligation is such that if there be no lawful cause to obstruct a marriage intended to be had and solemnized between the above bound Thomas Jefferson and Martha Skelton of the county of Charles city, widow, for which a licene is desired, then this obligation is to be null and void; otherwise to remain in full force.

The marriage banns for Martha Wayles Skelton and Thomas Jefferson when they were wed in 1772.

sure would almost certainly have made the Civil War impossible. It was one of many evidences of Jefferson's far-reaching vision and his hatred of human slavery. Three years later, in the Ordinance of 1787, chattel servitude was prohibited in the region northwest of the Ohio River.

Jefferson also was prevailed upon to serve with John Adams and Benjamin Franklin on the commission to negotiate peace, following the achievement of American independence in the Revolution. When this mission became unnecessary, he was named, with Adams and Franklin, to negotiate treaties of commerce. He accordingly sailed for France in 1784 with his eleven-year-old daughter Martha, usually known as Patsy, intending to remain for two years. The stay turned out to be for five and a half years. Father and daughter had been in Paris only a few months when the sad news came that another daughter, Lucy Elizabeth, aged two and a half, had died of whooping cough. Hence Jefferson's only child left in Virginia was Mary, known as Maria or Polly, and her father became increasingly determined to bring her to Paris, to be with him and her older sister.

However, it would be years before the journey to France could be arranged. Polly was nine when she finally arrived in 1787, accompanied by the fourteen-year-old slave girl Sally Hemings. Jefferson had asked for a more mature woman as Polly's companion and maid, but this had not been feasible. As mentioned, James Hemings, Sally's older brother, had traveled to Paris with the Jeffersons in 1784.

The presence of youthful Sally in the Parisian entourage seemed innocent enough, and apparently nobody at the time felt that it had any significance except the obvious one, that Sally was serving as Polly's companion. But Madison Hemings, a son born to Sally years later in Virginia, was to claim in 1873, long after both Sally and Jefferson were dead, that his mother became Jefferson's concubine and that she first became pregnant by her master in Paris. Mrs. Brodie has accepted this assertion as true. Its validity will be examined hereafter.

The Grille de Chaillot, looking toward Paris along the Champs-Elysées. The Hotel de Langeac, where Jefferson resided with his two daughters, was on the left, at the corner.

Jefferson was appointed minister to France in 1785, as successor to Franklin, and in that post he kept his finger on the course of events. The rumblings of the oncoming French revolution were ominous and alarming, although so great a friend of the masses as he could not fail to sympathize with them in their genuine grievances. Jefferson wrote of the "monstrous abuses under which the people were ground to powder," and he was not exaggerating. In a letter to James Madison in 1787 he also declared that "the king's passion for drink was divesting him of all respect, the queen was detested, and an explosion of some sort is not impossible." Two years later the Bastille fell (July 14, 1789), a few months before the Jeffersons returned to America, and Louis XVI and Marie Antoinette were on the road that would lead them ultimately to the guillotine. Jefferson was revolted by the excesses of the revolution, but he understood its causes better than most and was far more sympathetic to it than many Americans.

He had been diverted in 1786 from such serious concerns by his infatuation with Maria Cosway, the talented and charming wife of Richard Cosway, the most eminent English miniaturist of his time. Not much love was lost between the Cosways; Maria had apparently been talked into the marriage by her mother. Her husband is variously described as a fop and coxcomb who had affairs with other women and perhaps men.

Twenty-five letters between Thomas Jefferson and Maria Cosway suddenly surfaced in the 1940s in the papers of Jefferson's grandson, Thomas Jefferson Randolph. Jefferson had preserved them carefully, whereas he had destroyed his correspondence with his wife and his mother. It is obvious, therefore, that he did not object to their becoming available to posterity. Randolph apparently concluded in the nineteenth century that the time had not come to make them public, so he turned them over to his attorney and executor, in whose files they were found. Randolph, of course, could have destroyed them, but did not. They form the basis for the book *My Head and My Heart* by Helen Duprey Bullock.[4] Mrs. Brodie observes darkly that "most of the letters were kept hidden by Jefferson's heirs until the 1940s, . . ." implying some sort of conspiracy among a number of people, for which there is no evidence.[5]

Maria and Jefferson met in Paris in the autumn of 1786, and the forty-three-year-old widower, whose wife had died four years before, was attracted at once to the lovely twenty-seven-year-old woman with the golden hair and violet eyes. She was not only easy to look upon but greatly gifted both as an artist and a musician. At age nineteen she had been elected to the Academy of Fine Arts in Florence in her native Italy. (She was the daughter of a well-to-do English couple living there.) In the five years preceding her visit to Paris, she had had twenty-two paintings exhibited at London's Royal Academy. Maria played well on the harp and pianoforte, was also a composer, and had a fine singing voice. In addition she was an accomplished linguist. All of which could not fail to appeal to Jefferson, whose interests were quite similar. Malone says "there can be no doubt that he fell deeply in love during that golden September," and there appears to be no reason to question it. Whether there was "illicit love-making," no one knows. "If he as a widower ever engaged in it," says Malone, "this was the time."[6] Jefferson saw a great deal of Maria during these weeks until, when strolling with her one day in the Petit Cours he tried to jump a fence and fell. His right wrist was dislocated, and the excruciatingly painful injury not only prevented him from seeing her for a time, but forced him to learn to write with his left hand.

When she and her husband returned to London, he laboriously wrote her the famous letter "My Head and My Heart." In this extraordinary document he set forth at great length his struggles in determining whether his head or his heart was to have supremacy as he contemplated their re-

*Jefferson as a man of fashion in Paris, from a portrait by Mather Brown.
The figure in the background represents Liberty.*

Maria Cosway, from a portrait by Richard Cosway, engraved by L. Schiavonetti.

lationship. They corresponded intermittently thereafter, in words that, at times, would seem to imply a passionate love affair. However, given the romantic phraseology of that era, it appears that not too much importance should be attached to these seemingly torrid endearments—especially since by the time Maria returned alone to Paris for nearly four months the following year, there had been a mutual cooling of the inner fires. Such is the opinion of Dumas Malone, Merrill Peterson, Helen Bullock, Nathan Shachner, and Charles van Pelt.[7] But Fawn Brodie feels otherwise and says, without any documentation, that Maria "must certainly have been racked by fears of pregnancy." Brodie also interprets Maria's words "I cannot be useful to you" in her farewell note to Jefferson before departing for London as meaning that perhaps "there had been some kind of crucial failure in the act of love."[8] As with the reference to fears of pregnancy, this can only be pure supposition. There is no evidence that their relationship at that point involved fears of pregnancy or acts of love. On the contrary, there is reason to believe that if these things occurred, it was in the previous year.

They never saw each other again. Maria urged Jefferson in 1789 to stop over in London en route back to the United States, but he did not do so. He suggested that she visit America but seemed to discourage her from making the journey. Their subsequent correspondence was spasmodic. For example, in 1795 two letters arrived from Maria, who by that time had abandoned her husband. Jefferson did not reply for more than six months. Letters from her in 1823 and 1825, not long before his death, went unanswered.

Maria had always been religiously inclined, and her later correspondence with Jefferson was from a convent school for girls that she opened at Lodi, Italy. She spent the remainder of her days there and died in 1838. "In Milan and Lodi her death was regarded as a public calamity," Helen Bullock wrote in *My Head and My Heart*, "and her funeral was attended by members of the ·imperial family, by the dukes of all the neighboring municipalities and by many of the religious orders."

Why did Jefferson's affair with Maria cool off so abruptly, after it had begun so warmly in 1786? No one can say with certainty. Such a cooling happens to many lovers, for a variety of reasons. Mrs. Brodie is positive as to the explanation, namely that Jefferson began at that time his clandestine relationship with Sally and pretty well lost interest in Maria Cosway. "The evidence that the real rival was the comely little slave from Monticello, and that their affection began to bloom early in 1788, is complicated and subtle," she writes. Indeed it is; the real question is whether this "affection" ever existed.

Mrs. Brodie relies heavily on the statement given in 1873 by Madison Hemings, Sally's son, then living at Pee Pee, Pike County, Ohio, to the *Pike County Republican*. On its face, this declaration would seem to be convincing. The pertinent section follows:

Their stay [in Paris] (my mother and Maria's) was about eighteen months. But during that time my mother became Mr. Jefferson's concubine, and when he was called home she was *enciente* [sic] by him. He desired to bring my mother back to Virginia with him but she demurred. She was just beginning to understand the French language well, and in France she was free, while if she returned to Virginia she would be re-enslaved. So she refused to return with him. To induce her to do so he promised her extraordinary privileges, and made a solemn pledge that her children would be freed at the age of twenty-one years. In consequence of his promises, on which she implicitly relied, she returned with him to Virginia. Soon after their arrival she gave birth to a child, of whom Thomas Jefferson was the father. It lived but a short time. She gave birth to four others, and Jefferson was the father of all of them.[9]

A number of things about the foregoing arouse one's doubts and suspicions. In the first place, the entire interview, as published, is in language that a poorly educated ex-slave would almost certainly not have used. Mrs. Brodie says Madison Hemings's reminiscences in the *Pike County Republican* are "most competently related," though possibly "corrected by the editor who printed them."[10] It is more than a possibility that they were corrected; it is a virtual certainty. Consider the inclusion of the French word for "pregnant," *enceinte*—which, incidentally, was misspelled. Consider also the proficient use of English, more obvious in certain other passages than in the one quoted above. It sounds remarkably like the words of a newspaper editor or some other college-educated individual. Madison Hemings is quoted as saying, "I learned to read by inducing the white children to teach me the letters and something more; what else I know of books I have picked up here and there till now I can read and write." If all he learned was to read and write, where did that word *enceinte* come from, not to mention various other suspicious words and phrases?[11]

There are also numerous inaccuracies. Since Hemings was an elderly man in 1873, talking about events that occurred before he was born in 1805, this is hardly surprising. But when Hemings states that Jefferson "had but little taste or care for agricultural pursuits," it is as absurd as if he had said that Jefferson was not interested in the construction of Monticello. The *Farm Book*, *Garden Book*, and dozens of letters and other documents attest to Jefferson's consuming interest in all things agricultural. Mrs. Brodie does not mention this and other misstatements, but accepts Madison's assertions concerning Jefferson's relationship to Sally as gospel. On this latter point, Madison must have been simply relating what his mother or someone else told him concerning his parentage.

Note that in discussing Sally's supposed concubinage in Paris, he declared that the child she bore "soon after their arrival [in the United States] . . . lived but a short time."

Mrs. Brodie ignores the foregoing assertion and declares that Sally gave birth soon after her return to a son named Tom who, she said, lived to be at least ten or twelve years old, and then disappeared mysteriously from Monticello.[12] The first mention of this shadowy individual occurs in that authoritative journal the *Richmond Recorder* (September 1, 1802), edited by none other than James T. Callender. So we are indebted to Mrs. Brodie's "generally accurate reporter" for starting the crepuscular "Yellow Tom" on his mundane journey. Nobody has been able to nail him down or to prove that there was such a person. Brodie tries valiantly to trace Tom's movements after his supposed departure from Monticello. She mentions one tradition after another, admittedly uncertain as to whether any of them is correct. At one point she goes so far as to say, ". . . if he was, in truth, Jefferson and Sally Hemings's son . . ."[13] We are left with the strong impression that Tom was just another figment of Callender's fertile imagination. John C. Miller of the Stanford history faculty writes, "Callender credited 'Tom', whom he had never seen, with bearing a striking resemblance to the president. But no trace of the existence of 'Yellow Tom' has ever been discovered. . . . In actuality 'Yellow Tom' never existed." Winthrop D. Jordan agrees, as do Garry Wills, Merrill Peterson, and James Bear.[14]

Understandably then, various careful students have concluded that Sally Hemings was not pregnant with Tom or anyone else when she returned from Paris in 1789. One of these was the late Douglass Adair, former editor of the prestigious *William and Mary Quarterly*, who made an exhaustive examination of the relevant evidence. His comprehensive findings are published in his posthumous work, *Fame and the Founding Fathers*.

With Malone, Boyd, and Peterson, Adair points to Jefferson's extremely complete *Farm Book* as one piece of important evidence. In it the master of Monticello kept a careful record of slave births on his mountaintop through three generations. In this volume the births of Sally Hemings and her children are meticulously set down. There is no record of any child being born to her soon after her arrival from Paris in 1789. If Jefferson recorded the other children he is supposed to have fathered, why would he have omitted the first? According to the *Farm Book*, Sally's first child was born in 1795.

Furthermore, in order for us to credit the story of Sally's having a baby soon after her arrival from France, we must believe that Jefferson, a conspicuously loving father by all the credible evidence, seduced a sixteen-year-old slave girl and traveled with her on shipboard, in an advanced state of pregnancy, in the intimate company of his two young daughters. Anyone familiar with his relationship with his children, testified to by scores of affectionate letters and every proof of adoration and concern, will find such a story altogether unbelievable.

We should bear in mind also that in 1873, when Madison Hemings and the editor of the *Pike County Republican* collaborated on their statement, the Civil War had ended only a short time before, and many Northerners were engaged in trying to make the slave-holding South of antebellum days seem as abhorrent as possible.

Madison Hemings not only contended in his interview that Jefferson had seduced Madison's mother in Paris; he likewise claimed that even after Callender had exposed this supposedly clandestine relationship in 1802, Thomas Jefferson, then president of the United States, was so utterly brazen and unconcerned for public opinion that he fathered two more children by her while still in the presidency.

Julian Boyd says that Hemings's statement "was obviously prompted by someone . . . shaped and perhaps even written and embellished by the prompter." And Dumas Malone, calling attention to the atmosphere of the time, assigns it a place "in the tradition of political enmity and abolitionist propaganda." The *Pike County Republican* was edited by S. F. Wetmore, a native of Maine, who moved to Pike County after the Civil War and revived the local Republican paper. The rival Democratic journal was the *Waverly Watchman*. Both were published in the town of Waverly.

The *Waverly Watchman*, edited by John A. Jones, replied five days later (March 18, 1873) to the contentions attributed to Madison Hemings. Jones said, in part:

> We have no doubt but that there are at least fifty Negroes in this county who lay claim to illustrious parentage. . . . The children of Jefferson and Madison, Calhoun and Clay far outnumber Washington's body servants when Barnum was in the height of his prosperity. They are not to be blamed for making these assertions. It sounds much better for the mother to tell her offspring that 'master' is their father than to acknowledge to them that some field hand, without a name, had raised her to the dignity of a mother. . . . This is a well-known fact to those who have been reared in those states where slavery existed, and with them no attention whatever is paid to these rumors. . . . The fact that Hemings claims to be the natural son of Jefferson does not convince the world of its truthfulness.

Another reason why Sally may have told Madison that Jefferson was his father was that she wanted to protect the real father, who was a married man.

Near the end of 1873 (December 25) editor Wetmore returned to the attack in his paper. He had discovered another former Monticello slave, Israel Jefferson, who lived on Brushy Fork of Pee Pee Creek, Pebble Township. Israel submitted to an interview and was quoted as confirming Madison Hemings's claim that his mother was Thomas Jefferson's concubine, and that the author of the Declaration of Independence was the father of her children. "I can conscientiously confirm his [Madison's] statement as any other fact which I believe from circumstances but do not positively know," Israel is quoted as saying.

Saturday, March 22, 1873,

at three o'clock P. M. to nominate candidates
for township offices, to be supported at the
ensuing election on the 7th of April.

Also, to elect six delegates to a County
Convention, if one is called by the Central
Committee, to nominate for member to the
Constitutional Convention.

Let all the Republicans of the township be
present.   R. M. VINCENT, Ad. Com.

Life Among the Lowly.

NUMBER I.

MADISON HEMINGS.

I never knew of but one white man who
bore the name of Hemings; he was an Englishman and my greatgrandfather. He was
captain of an English trading vessel which
sailed between England and Williamsburg,
Va., then quite a port. My grandmother was
a fullblooded African, and possibly a native
of that country. She was the property of
John Wales, a Welchman. Capt. Hemings
happened to be in the port of Williamsburg
at the time my grandmother was born, and
acknowledging her fatherhood he tried to
purchase her of Mr. Wales, who would not
part with the child, though he was offered
an extraordinarily large price for her. She
was named Elizabeth Hemings. Being
thwarted in the purchase, and determining
to own his flesh and blood he resolved to
take the child by force or stealth, but the
knowledge of his intention coming to John
Wales ears, through leaky fellow servants
of the mother, she and the child were taken
into the "great house" under their master's
immediate care. I have been informed that
it was not the extra value of that child over
other slave children that induced Mr. Wales
to refuse to sell it, for slave masters then, as
in later days, had no compunctions of conscience which restrained them from part-
ing mother and child of however tender age,
but he was restrained by the fact that just
about that time amalgamation began, and
the child was so great a curiosity that its
owner desired to raise it himself that he
might see its outcome. Capt. Hemings soon
afterwards sailed from Williamsburg, never
to return. Such is the story that comes
down to me.

Elizabeth Hemings grew to womanhood
in the family of John Wales, whose wife
dying she (Elizabeth) was taken by the widower Wales as his concubine, by whom she
had six children—three sons and three
daughters, viz: Robert, James, Peter, Critty,
Sally and Thena. These children went by
the name of Hemings.

Williamsburg was the capital of Virginia,
and of course it was an aristocratic place,
where the "bloods" of the Colony and the
new State most did congregate. Thomas
Jefferson, the author of the Declaration of
Independence, was educated at William and

About his own house ....
.... He was kind ....
angry though sometimes he was irritated
when matters went wrong, but even then he
hardly ever allowed himself to be made unhappy any great length of time. Unlike
Washington he had but little taste or care
for agricultural pursuits. He left matters
pertaining to his plantations mostly with his
stewards and overseers. He always had
mechanics at work for him, such as carpen-
ters, blacksmiths, shoemakers, coopers, &c.
It was his mechanics he seemed mostly to
direct, and in their operations he took great
interest. Almost every day of his latter
years he might have been seen among them.
He occupied much of the time in his office
engaged in correspondence and reading and
writing. His general temperament was
smooth and even; he was very undemonstrative. He was uniformly kind to all
about him. He was not in the habit of showing partiality or fatherly affection to us
children. We were the only children of his
by a slave woman. He was affectionate
toward his white grandchildren, of whom
he had fourteen, twelve of whom lived to
manhood and womanhood. His daughter
Martha married Thomas Mann Randolph by
whom she had thirteen children. Two died
in infancy. The names of the living were
Ann, Thomas Jefferson, Ellen, Cornelia, Virginia, Mary, James, Benj. Franklin, Lewis
Madison, Septemia and Geo. Wythe. Thos.
Jefferson Randolph was Chairman of the
Democratic National Convention in Balti-
more last spring which nominated Horace
Greeley for the Presidency, and Geo. Wythe
Randolph was Jeff. Davis' first Secretary of
War in the late "unpleasantness."

Maria married John Epps, and raised one
on—Francis.

My father generally enjoyed excellent
health. I never knew him to have but one
spell of sickness, and that was caused by a
visit to the Warm Springs in 1818. Till
within three weeks of his death he was hale
and hearty, and at the age of 83 years he
walked erect and with stately tread. I am
now 68, and I well remember that he was a
much smarter man physically, even at that
age, than I am.

When I was fourteen years old I was put
to the carpenter trade under the charge of
John Hemings, the youngest son of my
grandmother. His father's name was Nelson,
who was an Englishman. She had seven
children by white men and seven by colored
men—fourteen in all. My brothers, sister
Harriet and myself were used alike. They
were put to some mechanical trade at the
age of fourteen. Till then we were permitted to stay about the "great house," and
only required to do such light work as going
on errands. Harriet learned to spin and
to weave in a little factory on the home
plantation. We were free from the dread of
having to be slaves all our lives long, and
were measurably happy. We were always
permitted to be with our mother, who was
well used. It was her duty, all her life

The Waverly (Ohio) Pike County Republican *for March 13, 1873,
weekly newspaper containing an interview with elderly Madison Hemings in
which he claimed that Jefferson was his father, without producing any
evidence.*

Waverly Watchman.

JOHN A. JONES — Editor

TUESDAY, MARCH 18, 1873.

• Life Among the Lowly

The editor of the "Republican" having nothing of a weighty character on his hands, has commenced the publication of a series of articles entitled, "Life Among the Lowly," or the Lives and Adventures of Illegitimate Sons of Illustrious Sires, the first installment of which appears in the last issue of that paper. Madison Hemings heads the list, claiming to be the natural son of Thomas Jefferson by an illegitimate daughter of John Wales, the father in law of Jefferson.

Hemings, or rather Wetmore, gives a very truthful account of the public and private life of the Jefferson family; but this no doubt, was condensed from one of the numerous lives of Jefferson which can be found in any well regulated family library. We have no doubt but there are at least fifty negroes in this county who lay claim to illustrious parentage. This is a well known peculiarity of the colored race. The children of Jefferson and Madison, Calhoun and Clay far out number Washington's body servants when Barnum was in the height of his prosperity. They are not to be blamed for making these assertions. It sounds much better for the mother to tell her offspring that "master" is their father than to acknowledge to them that some field hand, without a name, had raised her to the dignity of a mother. They want the world to think they are particular in their liaisons with the stern er sex, whether the truth will bear them out or not. This is a well-known fact to those who have been

whatever, is paid to these rumors.— If they were, the "master" would have to bear the odium of all the licentious practices that are developed on the plantation. The fact that Hemings claims to be the natural son of Jefferson does not convince the world of its truthfulness. He is not supposed to be a competent witness in his own behalf. He was no doubt present at the time of accouchment, but his extreme youth would prevent him from knowing all the facts connected with that important event.— Jefferson was over 62 years of age when Hemings appeared upon the sacred soil of Virginia, if we are to believe his biographer. The extreme age of Jefferson, coupled with his natural frigidity of constitution causes a doubt in our mind whether or not Hemings has been correctly informed about the author of his being. Solomon, (if we have been corectly informed) said, when he took his two hundredth wife, "it's a wise child that knows its own father."— The same is as true to-day as it was in lays of Solomon. At all events, Jefferson is not here to put in a disclaimer, and we think it rather mean to ake this advantage of the author of the Declaration of Independence.

A perusal of Hemings' autobiography reminds us of the pedigree printed on the numerous stud-horse bills that can be seen posted around during the Spring season. No matter how scrubby the stock or whether he horse has any known pedigree, he "Horse Owner" furnishes a full and complete pedigree of every celebrated horse in the country. One of hese is copied, and the scrawniest 'plng" rejoices in a descent that would put Sir Archy to shame. The horse is not expected to know what is claimed for him. But we have often thought if one of them could read and would happen to come across his pedigree, tacked conspicuously at a prominent cross road, he

COURTESY OF THE VIRGINIA STATE LIBRARY

The Waverly Watchman *for March 18, 1873 with that paper's scornful retort to the* Pike County Republican's *issue of five days before, containing Madison Hemings's claim that Jefferson was his father.*

Mrs. Brodie concedes that "the reminiscences of Israel Jefferson . . . are written in so similar a style [to those of Madison Hemings] as to suggest that both memoirs were written by the same newspaperman after the interviews with these ex-slaves."[15]

This is obvious when we note that Israel, like Madison, was able to do hardly more than read and write. Israel said in the aforementioned interview, "Since I have been in Ohio I have learned to read and write, but my duties as a laborer would not permit me to acquire much of an education." Yet consider the following sample of his prose, as recorded by Wetmore:

Since my residence in Ohio I have several times visited Monticello. My last visit was in the fall of 1866. Near there I found the same [Thomas] Jefferson Randolph, whose service as administrator I left more than forty years ago, at Monticello. He had grown old, and was outwardly surrounded by the evidences of former ease and opulence gone to decay. He was in poverty. He had lost, he told me, $80,000 in money by joining the South in rebellion against the government. Except his real estate, the rebellion stripped him of everything, save one old blind mule. He said that if he had taken the advice of his sister, Mrs. Colleridge [Coolidge], gone to New York and remained there during the war, he could have saved the bulk of his property. But he was a rebel at heart, and chose to go with his people. Consequently, he was served as others had been—he had lost all his servants and nearly all his personal property of every kind. I went back to Virginia to find the proud and haughty Randolph in poverty, at Edge Hill, within four miles of Monticello, where he was bred and born. Indeed, I then realized more than ever before, the great changes which time brings about in the affairs and circumstances of life.

Like Madison Hemings, Israel Jefferson made a number of inaccurate statements. He said he had been born on Christmas day, "the year I suppose was 1797," and "my earliest recollections are the exciting events attending the preparation of Mr. Jefferson and other members of his family on their removal to Washington" for his presidential inauguration. The *Farm Book* shows that Israel was born in 1800, not 1797. The Jeffersons moved to Washington in late 1800 or early 1801. Israel either hadn't been born or was a newly arrived baby. Hence his "recollections" are among the most precocious on record.

Israel also refers to Lafayette's visit to Monticello in 1824, saying that the Frenchman "remained with Mr. Jefferson six weeks, and almost every day I took them out to drive." Actually Lafayette was at Monticello only ten days.[16]

So much for the contention of Israel Jefferson and Madison Hemings that Thomas Jefferson was the father of Sally Hemings's children. It seems clear that their claims are subject to serious reservations and have many vulnerabilities.

In addition to the evidence that Mrs. Brodie finds in the words of James Callender and Madison Hemings to support her thesis that Jefferson had a thirty-eight-year relationship with Sally Hemings, there are her psychological interpretations. These are rejected out of hand by many historians, but they permeate her biography.

For example, Jefferson made a seven-week tour of several European countries in 1788 and kept a diary. "Anyone who reads with care these twenty-five pages must find it singular that in describing the countryside . . . he used the word mulatto' eight times," writes Mrs. Brodie. He was describing the color of the soil. On a tour in the previous year he had used the term "mulatto" only once, she says.[17]

There are also her references to the shape of the plough and the women he saw in the fields. "Considering the ancient symbolism of the plough," writes Brodie, "it is not surprising, perhaps, that writing about the ideal shape of this ancient and basic agricultural tool led him immediately to observations about the women he had seen in the fields who followed close behind it." Mrs. Brodie does not elaborate upon the "ancient symbolism of the plough," and we are left in the dark as to just what this symbolism is. One is reminded of her cryptic reference (page 79) to the fig's "ancient symbolic history, relating to both love and sin," apropos of Jefferson's action in sending a basket of figs to the dying John Walker in 1809.

At all events, she quotes Jefferson as follows concerning the women he saw in the fields on his European tour:

> The women here . . . do all sorts of work. While one considers them as useful and rational companions, one cannot forget that they are also the objects of our pleasures. Nor can they ever forget it. While employed in dirt and drudgery some tag of ribbon, some ring or bit of bracelet, carbob or necklace, or something of that kind will shew that the desire of pleasing is never suspended in them. . . . They are formed by nature for attentions and not for hard labor.

Mrs. Brodie concludes from the foregoing: "This is all very tender and suggests that he was thinking not at all about the splendidly dressed Maria Cosway when he wrote it."[18]

Equally far-fetched is Brodie's interpretation of Jefferson's letter to Maria upon his return to Paris: "He described briefly his trip to Germany, with a glowing description of the art gallery at Düsseldorf. Here, in describing the painting that excited him above all others, he betrayed, inadvertently as a man often does to an old love, that he had been captured by a new one." The extract from his letter follows:

> At Dusseldorp I wished for you much. I surely never saw so precious a collection of paintings. Above all things

those of Van der Werff affected me the most. His picture of Sarah delivering Agar to Abraham is delicious. I would have agreed to have been Abraham though the consequence would have been that I should have been dead five or six thousand years. . . . I am but a son of nature, loving what I see and feel, without being able to give a reason, nor caring much whether there be one.

Mrs. Brodie then affords us the following insight into Jefferson's true meaning:

"Agar"—Hagar the Egyptian—it will be remembered was Abraham's concubine, given to him by his wife Sarah when she could not bear a child, and destined to become the legendary mother of the Arab peoples. In this painting she is pictured as very young, partly nude, but seductive in a fashion that is innocence itself. She is blond, with long straight hair down her back. Abraham, though bearded, is far from old, with the nude shoulders and chest of a young and vigorous giant. . .

Although Jefferson included tender passages in this letter to Maria Cosway . . . he confessed callously that he had found it impossible to write a letter to her on the whole seven-week journey. "At Strasbourg I sat down to write you," he admitted. "But for my soul I could think of nothing at Strasbourg but the promontory of noses, of Diego, of Slawkenburgius the historian, and the procession of Strasburgers to meet the man with the nose. . . ."

"Maria Cosway was not only baffled but enraged," writes Brodie. " 'How could you led me by the hand all the way [Cosway, as a native of Italy, wrote awkward English] think of me, have Many things to say, and not find One word to write *but on Noses?*' "

And Brodie provides us with the following truly extraordinary interpretation:

> One may well echo Maria Cosway's question, "Why noses?" As we have already asked. "Why mulatto?" Jefferson's bemusement with the one may well have been related to the other. If Sally Hemings, though "mighty near white," retained a suggestion of her grandmother's physical heritage in the shape of her nose, it could be that Jefferson, caught up in a new passion, was cursing the world's insistence on caring about such matters. Though his preoccupation with this girl of mixed blood did not cost him a city, as did the preoccupation of the Strasbourgers with a nose, it would eventually threaten to cost him the presidency. [19]

Mrs. Brodie mentions all this as though it had some profound significance, a significance that will, we daresay, escape most readers. Furthermore, she refers to an imaginary "threat to his presidency." Evidence of this "threat" is hard to find; indeed it appears to be nonexistent. Malone says Jefferson's "political position had never seemed more secure than in the autumn of 1804 [two years following Callender's "revelations"], for it was then that he was triumphantly reelected"—in a landslide. [20]

We come next to Brodie's discovery that in mentioning an orangutan in a letter to Maria Cosway, Jefferson inadvertently let the monkey out of the bag with respect to Sally Hemings. January 1789 was one of the coldest Januaries on record in Paris, for carriages were crossing the Seine on the ice. "Surely it was never so cold before," Jefferson wrote. "To me who am an animal of a warm climate, a mere Oran-ootan, it has been a severe trial." Mrs. Brodie comments:

> We do not know exactly what Jefferson conceived an "Oran-ootan" to be, but we do know that in his *Notes*

on the State of Virginia, published only a few months
before Sally Hemings's arrival, he had indiscreetly written that blacks preferred whites over their own species,
just as the "Oran-ootan" preferred "the black woman over
those of his own species." That he may now suddenly
have become uneasy about what he had written concerning this mysterious man of nature, or man of the
woods, is suggested by the fact that on Oct. 2, 1788,
when he sent away to his London bookdealer for a
list of books for purchase, he included E. Tyson's *Oran-
outang: or, An Anatomy of a Pigmy* (1699). . . . Jefferson
had good reason to be uncomfortable. For when the
Federalist press in America later heard rumors about his
slave paramour, the editors needled him cruelly on this
very passage in his *Notes*. [21]

Just what all this proves may have been clear to Mrs. Brodie,
but it leaves many others baffled.

She writes (page 233) that "there is also what one might
call hard evidence that Jefferson in Paris treated Sally Hemings with special consideration." It seems that he paid 240
francs for a smallpox inoculation for Sally, "a very great sum."
So it was, but if Jefferson didn't want an outbreak of the
disease in his entourage, what alternative did he have? James
Bear says the figure "most probably included room and board
for the six weeks or more period of quarantine."[22] Mrs. Brodie
mentions that a French tutor was engaged for Sally, apparently Monsieur Perrault, who was also tutoring James. The
latter was evidently a trial for the gentleman, who sought on
one occasion to collect for his services during the preceding
twenty months only to be punched and kicked by James, who
tore Perrault's only overcoat. Small wonder that the tutor, in
remonstrating to Jefferson, complained of *"sotisses les plus durs"*
("most frightful stupidities").[23] No doubt Jefferson saw that
the bill was paid. As for wages, James and Sally were on an
equal footing—each was paid 24 francs a month, beginning in

1788. Brodie tells us that in 1789 Jefferson suddenly began spending "a surprising amount of money on Sally's clothes." However, the outlays for Patsy's clothes were "several times" as much. Since Jefferson, as United States ambassador, was moving in the highest circles in France, it is hardly to be expected that his daughter's companion would under any circumstances have been shoddily dressed. The record as to these expenditures "seems to have been kept as secret as possible," says Brodie, without offering any evidence.

And there are those missing letters of Jefferson's for "this critical year of 1788 . . . the only volume missing in the whole forty-three-year epistolary record." Among the communications that disappeared were letters that he wrote his daughters. "This raises the question whether or not someone at some time went through Jefferson's papers systematically eliminating every possible reference to Sally Hemings," writes the ever-suspicious Mrs. Brodie. (Why, then, were the daughters' letters also "eliminated"?) Letters from Jefferson to Sally's brothers and from her brothers to him are extant. But no letters or notes exchanged between Sally Hemings and Thomas Jefferson have as yet found their way into the public record. One explanation could be that there never were any. As David Herbert Donald, the Pulitzer Prize–winning Harvard historian, wrote in reviewing Brodie's Jefferson biography for *Commentary:* "Mrs. Brodie is masterful in using negative evidence. . . . The fact that Jefferson's *Farm Book*, in which he scrupulously itemized all his expenses, shows that he gave no favorite treatment to Sally and her offspring can only mean that he was surreptiously slipping her the money that he listed under 'Charity'."

A new situation presents itself, Donald points out, "when there is no evidence whatever to cloud her [Brodie's] vision," for then "she is free to speculate."

"It seems likely . . . One can only guess . . ." she begins a paragraph describing Sally's feelings upon returning from

France to America and to slavery. "No one can know," she says of Jefferson's sentiments on this occasion—and then proceeds to reveal in detail what he must have felt. Where there are no troublesome documents, Mrs. Brodie can offer proof by coincidence: is it not significant that Jefferson's daughter decided to become a nun during the same month that he ordered some clothing for his slave Sally? And is it not even more revealing that another Jefferson daughter married and left home shortly after Sally gave birth to one of her numerous children? In the absence of any reference to Sally in all the letters of Jefferson and his daughters, does not silence constitute overwhelming evidence that the daughters knew all about the affair with the slave girl and disapproved of it?

We continue with examples of Mrs. Brodie's psychological approach to the doings of the wayward Mr. Jefferson.

During the latter's affair with Mrs. Cosway in Paris, John Trumbull, the portrait painter, wrote him from London that Mrs. Cosway's husband and various of her friends were annoyed that they had not received a single line from her in three weeks. Jefferson replied, in part, to Trumbull, "So many infidelities in the postoffice are complained of since the rumors of war have arisen that I have waited a safer opportunity of enclosing you a bill of exchange." Mrs. Brodie comments, "Here, it would seem, he came very close to saying what was really bothering him—*So many complaints of our infidelities are coming through the postoffice.*"[25]

Upon returning to Monticello in 1794 from service in Washington's cabinet, Jefferson wrote several letters expressing his intense pleasure at once more experiencing the joys of rural life. To a French friend he declared, "I have returned with infinite appetite to the enjoyment of my farm, my family and my books." To John Adams he wrote, "I return to farming with an ardor that I scarcely knew in my youth," and to James Madison, "I find my mind totally absorbed in my rural occupations." Mrs. Brodie, with Sally Hemings on her mind, comes up with the following exegesis: "Infinitely the happier, totally absorbed, ardor, infinite appetite—these are strong words, with the unmistakable flavor of sexuality. They suggest that satisfactions of the body at Monticello were real."[26] Which led David Donald to observe in his review that Brodie "appears to be a disciple of the late A. C. Kinsey and believes that a man should be judged by the fullness and frequency of his sex life." He adds: "She ought to have given her book a better title. Why not 'By Sex Obsessed?' " Pursuing this theme further, Donald observes, apropos of her interpretation of Jefferson's reference in his John Trumbull letter to "infidelities of the postoffice," "One presumes that when Jefferson wrote Ralph Izard about 'infidelities of the postoffice' he was giving a hint of homosexual passion that Mrs. Brodie has inexcusably overlooked."

A parenthetical reference in Jefferson's famous letter to James Madison from Paris in 1789, in which Jefferson enunciated his view that "the earth belongs in usufruct to the living,"[27] is interpreted by Mrs. Brodie as signifying that Jefferson was thinking of Sally Hemings. His experience as minister to France "destroyed any lingering puritanical legacy from his childhood," she says, "broadened his compassion for anyone caught up in the delights and difficulties of extramarital adventure, and confirmed his private conviction that a man is master of his own body and may govern it as he pleases." In considering this lengthy communication, covering several pages and devoted to a serious discussion of "political relativism" and the question whether "one generation of men has a right to bind another," with special emphasis on "the power of contracting debts," Mrs. Brodie focuses on a single brief sentence. Jefferson wrote Madison from Paris, in part, as follows: "The earth belongs always to the living generation. They may manage it, then, and what proceeds from it, as they please, during their usufruct. *They are masters, too, of their own persons, and consequently may govern them as they please* [italics

Jean Antoine Houdon's exceptionally fine bust of Jefferson, made from life in 1789, and exhibited at the Paris Salon; now in the Boston Museum of Fine Arts.

supplied]. But persons and property make the sum of the objects of government. The institutions and laws of their predecessors extinguished them in their natural course with those who gave them being. . . ." Mrs. Brodie leaps upon the foregoing italicized statement and provides this comment (pages 186, 244–245): "Almost none of this was obvious in his own time, and is evident today only if one scrutinizes letters which Jefferson's heirs for many years took pains to hide. Here if anywhere one finds the answer to the question whether Jefferson embraced the monastic and continent life ascribed to him by so many, or whether his vital sexuality, instead of atrophying, reasserted itself to make possible a new, if hidden happiness."

To support the foregoing sweeping assertion, Mrs. Brodie provides no evidence at all, except a footnote calling attention to Jefferson's above-quoted letter to Madison. In her reiterated reference to "letters which Jefferson's heirs for many years took pains to hide," she apparently has in mind the letters between Jefferson and Maria Cosway, in which Sally Hemings is nowhere mentioned, and which seem temporarily to have been pigeonholed by Jefferson's grandson; and the letter from Ellen Coolidge, his granddaughter, to her husband, which was not released for publication in its entirety until 1974. This latter communication, far from supporting Mrs. Brodie's contentions as to Jefferson's supposed miscegenation, provides some of the most striking evidence as to their incorrectness. (see Chapter 6.) Upon such gauzy foundations Mrs. Brodie erects far-reaching conclusions as to the reassertion by Jefferson of his "vital sexuality."

A still more extraordinary interpretation comes to us on page 284 of her Jefferson biography. Edwin M. Yoder, Jr., commenting in *National Review*, (May 10, 1974), on this passage, makes the following observation: "Of all these strained speculations the prize must surely be given to her suggestion that when Jefferson decided to remodel Monticello after his sojourn in France, 'the possibility can be suggested that since buildings often symbolize in dreams the body of a woman, Jefferson . . . may have been unconsciously defining and redefining his ideal woman.' " Yoder goes on to say, "It can be suggested also that Jefferson, who tinkered with his house and grounds constantly for some forty years, wanted to incorporate the new architectural ideas he had garnered in Europe."

There is also Brodie's interpretation of Jefferson's *Syllabus of an Estimate of the Doctrines of Jesus*, which she says is "generally described simply as a defense against the continuing public libel that he was an atheist," but is actually "much more an attempt at a resolution of a shattering personal dilemma." She goes on to state that "his affection for Sally Hemings, and hers for him, long a private and inoffensive secret, had been turned into political pornography." Mrs. Brodie then says, "So Jefferson began his syllabus with a curious sentence: 'In a comparative view of the Ethics of the enlightened nations of antiquity, of the Jews and of Jesus, no notice should be taken of the corruptions of reason among the ancients, to wit, the idolatry and superstition of the vulgar, nor of the corruptions of Christianity by the learned among its professors." The fact that there is anything "curious" about the foregoing sentence had indeed escaped the attention of the leading students of Jefferson's thought processes and religious beliefs. Unfortunately these students were males, and hence not equipped with the "feeling" and "nuance" which, according to Mrs. Brodie, are vouchsafed only to women—males, it appears, are incapable of understanding "Jefferson and the life of the heart." So she provides us with the true explanation. "Could the repetition of the word 'corruption' suggest that he was not so much contemplating the 'corruptions of Christianity' or the 'corruptions of reason' as the corruptions of Thomas Jefferson?" she asks. "That he was defensive and anxious shows not only in the document itself but also in the letters accompanying it, which he sent to his daughters and Benjamin Rush." He wrote Martha that he was placing "my religious creed on paper," and that he wished his family to have the syllabus, so that they might be able to "estimate the libels published against me on this, as on every other possible subject." Jefferson wrote Benjamin Rush in similar vein, saying that he felt no obligation to any "inquisition over the rights of conscience," since questions of faith were a private matter "between God and himself." Brodie adds, incomprehensibly, "So, too, he seems to have been saying, were questions of the heart."[28]

On such foundations she has erected her case for the grave charges she has brought against Thomas Jefferson.

5

Fiction Masquerading
as Fact

In 1979 publication of Barbara Chase-Riboud's novel *Sally
Hemings* brought to public notice once more the legends
concerning Sally Hemings and Thomas Jefferson. The book,
an example of what today is sometimes termed "faction"
rather than fiction, was not only a Literary Guild selection,
but the author was accorded a vast amount of publicity in
interviews across the country as she traveled from city to city
promoting her novel. In these interviews, as in the book, she
stated flatly that Jefferson had fathered Sally Hemings's
mulatto children.

In advertising the novel, Viking Press, its publishers,
said, "The family tried to hide it. The history books tried to
ignore it. But the passionate, complex affair between Thomas
Jefferson and his mistress and slave Sally Hemings is the story
that had to be told."[1]

The Viking Press catalog for 1979 (page 49) declared,
"While most documents related to that passion were carefully
destroyed by Jefferson's white family after his death, enough
remained to substantiate the basic facts of the case." Dumas
Malone protested in a letter dated January 19, 1979, that
"this unsupported assertion is utterly irresponsible," and "it
is entirely incorrect to say that documents exist which substantiate the story." He added that "no serious student of

Jefferson can agree with this statement." As a result, the claim as to the destruction of documents by the family was not used by Viking in subsequent advertising.

Mrs. Chase-Riboud was born Barbara Chase in Philadelphia. After studying art and architecture at Yale University she went to London to work as a sculptor. She then removed to Paris, where she met and married the French photographer Mark Riboud. At the time of the publication of her novel they had been married sixteen years and had two sons. As for her own "racial mix," Mrs. Chase-Riboud said in an interview with Flora Lewis in the *New York Times* (October 22, 1979), "I had a Scottish great-grandfather, some English or Irish, some Indian, probably some Hindu and whatever there was in the Caribbean. I look a lot like my mother. Father is darker. My paternal aunt and grandmother are very white. . . ."

After the publication of *Sally Hemings*, the fact that a woman of mixed race claimed that there had been a thirty-eight-year relationship between one of the greatest Americans and a black slave seemed to intrigue the press. Columns and columns of space were accorded Mrs. Chase-Riboud. One would have supposed she had discovered some highly significant unknown truth concerning Thomas Jefferson, whereas she was in fact alleging something to have occurred that the leading authorities have always regarded as a myth.

Chase-Riboud freely conceded that she learned of these charges as to Jefferson from Fawn Brodie's biography. She had never heard of them before. Also, in the course of research for the novel, she sustained what she termed "one of the biggest shocks of my life." This was occasioned by her discovery of "the proposed anti-slavery clause in the Declaration of Independence," in which Jefferson scathingly denounced the slave trade and King George III of Great Britain for promoting it. The clause was stricken from the Declaration before its adoption because of objections by delegates to the Continental Congress, especially those from far southern colonies. Why the discovery of this paragraph was a serious shock to Chase-Riboud is not altogether clear. Students of the period are entirely familiar with it. Jefferson had expressed some of the same ideas in his *Summary View of the Rights of British America*, written in 1774 as instructions to the Virginia delegates to the Continental Congress of that year, but also deemed too radical. Furthermore, the deletion of the paragraph from the Declaration of Independence was dramatically portrayed in the recent popular musical *1776*. Yet Mrs. Chase-Riboud declares, "It's a mystery why historians have virtually hidden from the American public one of the most important clauses of the document as Jefferson originally wrote it."

The foregoing quotations from Chase-Riboud occur in a release from her publishers. She also asserted there that "the very idea that Sally Hemings was Jefferson's mistress for thirty-eight years evokes violent passions and prejudices." In an interview with the *Chicago Tribune* (July 3, 1979), which consumed several columns, she observed that "no one gets hysterical when you mention the mistresses of Goethe or Tolstoy," which, she said, is in contrast to the attitude of leading Jefferson biographers with respect to Sally Hemings.

It would be interesting to know when those biographers waxed "hysterical" over the Sally Hemings allegations or evidenced "violent passions and prejudices." Not only are these scholars unhysterical; they do not categorically deny the truth of the charges, although Chase-Riboud refers to "pages and pages of categorical denials." All that the leading Jeffersonians say is that the charges are in all probability false. By contrast, Fawn Brodie and Barbara Chase-Riboud are decidedly categorical in saying, on flimsy evidence, that there was beyond all question a prolonged sexual relationship between Jefferson and his slave.

Consider the following calm words from Dumas Malone:

The miscegenation story, as elaborated after Jefferson's death, assigned to him the paternity of the children borne by Sally Hemings during his presidency, two of them in his second term. He was even accused of casting out, toward the end of his life, an allegedly beautiful mulatto daughter and forcing her into a life of shame. The latter charge can be disproved by testimony and information now available. The former assumed that, despite the publicity Callender and the Federalist newspapers gave his alleged liaison, he continued it during his sixties while holding the highest office in the land, thus defying public opinion and wholly disregarding the feelings of his beloved daughters and grandchildren. To charge him with that degree of imprudence and insensitivity requires extraordinary credulity. . . . Quite obviously the truth must be sought in the life he actually lived, not in what political enemies or social reformers have said about that life for their own purposes, good or bad.[2]

And here is Merrill Peterson's analysis of the charges:

Sally . . . had accompanied Polly to Paris in 1787. After her return she had a number of children, all light skinned, whose paternity some wanton men ascribed to Jefferson. Like most legends this one was not created out of the whole cloth. The evidence, highly circumstantial, is far from conclusive, however, and unless Jefferson was capable of slipping badly out of character in hidden moments at Monticello, it is difficult to imagine him caught up in a miscegenous relationship. Such a mixture of the races, such a ruthless exploitation of the master-slave relationship, revolted his whole being.[3]

Historians of the caliber of Malone and Peterson are interested in facts, whether they reflect favorably or unfavorably upon the individual about whom they are writing. Goethe and Tolstoy may well have had mistresses, as Chase-Riboud said. This would seem to differentiate their cases sharply from that of Jefferson, who in all likelihood never had a mistress. Furthermore, he issued what can be interpreted as a blanket denial, although Mrs. Brodie thinks not. His private letter to his friend Secretary of the Navy Smith, admitting that he made improper advances to Mrs. John Walker in his youth, also contained the words "It is the only one founded on truth among all their allegations against me." Mrs. Brodie contends that since the letter to Smith was directed specifically to the Mrs. Walker matter, and Sally Hemings was not mentioned, Jefferson was not denying the charges involving her.[4] Possibly so, but the word "all" covers considerable territory. Countless charges against him, involving Sally Hemings, had been made and published in the preceding years, and he could well have had these in mind in his sweeping denial.

A paperback edition of Chase-Riboud's *Sally Hemings*, published by Avon, appeared in 1980, with lurid promotion. The following language was used by Avon in *Publishers Weekly* advertising: "She was the mistress of a president's estate. The mother of his children. And the slave he wouldn't free. Now Barbara Chase-Riboud tells the story of SALLY HEMINGS, the woman Thomas Jefferson couldn't live without when the scandal almost cost him the presidency."

You can't be much more categorical than that, in contrast to those quoted above who question the authenticity of the story but are far less categorical. There are at least four highly questionable and unprovable statements in that paragraph, and each is made as though it were an unchallenged fact. There was also the announcement that there would be a "provocative 30-second television commercial . . . in major markets, backed by print advertising in the June *Cosmopolitan*." This latter advertisement said, among other things, "By day she wore the keys to Monticello; by night she stole secretly to his arms."

What of Barbara Chase-Riboud's "faction" as a literary achievement? There were varied opinions. Its selection by the

Literary Guild would seem to testify to its quality, if we may assume that the mass market book clubs are always primarily interested in quality rather than sales appeal. Reviewers praised the work highly as "a sensitive, elegant and informative novel," and "a wise and compassionate book," and the University of Rochester awarded it the Kafka Prize as 1979's best work of fiction by an American woman. On the other hand, it was severely criticized as loaded with anachronisms, and critics declared that "the history itself is thin" and "at its best the novel is ordinary." As a first adventure in novel writing by an author not schooled in the history of the period, *Sally Hemings* may be said to have been a reasonably creditable performance, if one overlooks the basic fact that its entire theme is founded on completely unproven assumptions as to Thomas Jefferson's relationship with one of his slaves.

"The historical verity of the love affair is less important to me than its symbolic, almost mythical dimensions," Barbara Chase-Riboud is quoted as saying in a Viking Press release. "My Sally Hemings is not the historical Sally Hemings." In her interview with the *New York Times* this theme is elaborated upon. Chase-Riboud is concerned with "the metaphysics of race," and she concludes that "The U.S. is a mulatto country," which Ms. Lewis, her interviewer, says is the "underlying theme of the book." Jeffersonian historians have been "raging" about the novel because they feel "it compromises Jefferson in terms of race and color in America, since he was the man who he was," said Chase-Riboud. (Ah, those "raging historians"!)

Flora Lewis declared unequivocally in the course of the interview that Sally Hemings "became the mistress of Thomas Jefferson," and observed that the historical research for the Chase-Riboud novel "is substantial and convincing." A reviewer asserts that "Riboud follows meticulously not just the history of the times, but the psychology."

In point of fact, the book contains serious inaccuracies.

Sally is made to say (page 247), "If they really want to hear about Southern gentlemen and Negro mistresses we . . . can start with John Marshall, the chief justice of the United States." This is the sort of charge that is brought against great Americans without the slightest supporting evidence. Marshall's tender love for his wife, Polly, extended over their entire married life of nearly fifty years and into his old age. It is one of the most moving love stories in our history.

Chase-Riboud has James Hemings, one of the Hemings slaves, say (page 182) that he called Jefferson "to his face, if no strangers are present, TJ or Jefferson." Those who believe that will believe anything.

There are a number of careless misspellings and similar errors. For example, Jefferson's nephew Dabney Carr appears several times as Danby Carr. John Wickham, the celebrated defender of Aaron Burr in his trial for treason, is called George Wickham, and the Rivanna River near Monticello is spelled Ravina. James T. Callender appears thus at one point and as Thomas T. Callender at another. Monticello is described on page 232 as forty miles from Chesapeake Bay and on page 317 as two hundred miles away. Edgehill, the well-known home of the Randolphs almost in the shadow of Monticello, is said to have been forty miles from Jefferson's mountaintop (page 199). The Virginia General Assembly is twice referred to as the House of Burgesses (pages 13 and 311) long after that term, used in the colonial era, had been abandoned.

There is a strange incongruity in the language attributed to Elizabeth Hemings, Sally's mother, in her conversations with Sally (pages 25–33). In the first couple of pages she is made to speak almost grammatically, but she then lapses suddenly into such expressions as "we was," "they was," and "he could hear them boards creaking."

Since Chase-Riboud is not a historian, some of the foregoing lapses may be pardoned.

In her behalf, it should be said that the love scenes between Jefferson and Sally are told with definite restraint. The author could have gone to the bedroom and described episodes of delirious passion. To her credit, she did not do this, and we should all be grateful.

The basic criticism to be made of the novel *Sally Hemings*, of course, is that the fundamental assumption around which it revolves is spurious. The strong probability is that Thomas Jefferson and Sally Hemings had only the most conventional and proper relationship.

6

Enter
the Carr Brothers

If Thomas Jefferson did not father Sally Hemings's brood of illegitimates at Monticello, who did? There is an entirely plausible answer, much more plausible than the unsupported speculations of those who attribute the paternity of these individuals to Jefferson.

Much evidence points to Peter and Samuel Carr, Jefferson's nephews, sons of his sister Martha and Dabney Carr. Sally Hemings and her equally light-skinned niece Betsey each had a number of children, and it is not altogether certain which of the nephews was the father of Sally's brood and which of Betsey's. In any event, it seems clear that one or the other sired the children that Sally Hemings bore, about whom there has been such controversy down the years.

Some of the most convincing evidence is contained in a conversation between Thomas J. Randolph, Jefferson's grandson, and Henry S. Randall, the Jefferson biographer already mentioned. The conversation is described in a letter dated June 1, 1868 from Randall to James Parton, another Jefferson biographer.[1] The letter said, in part:

> Walking about mouldering Monticello one day with Col.
> T. J. Randolph . . . he showed me a smoke blackened

Thomas Jefferson Randolph, Jefferson's grandson, shown at age sixteen in a hitherto unpublished portrait by Charles Willson Peale, which hangs at Monticello.

and sooty room in one of the collonades and informed me it was Sally Henings' [*sic*] room. He asked me if I knew how the story of Mr. Jefferson's connection with her originated. I told him I did not. "There was a better excuse for it," said he, "than you might think: she had children that resembled Mr. Jefferson so closely that it was plain that they had his blood in their veins." He said in one case the resemblance was so close, that at some distance or in the dusk, the slave dressed in the same way, might have been mistaken for Mr. Jefferson. . . .

Col. Randolph informed me that Sally Henings was the mistress of Peter [Carr] and her sister Betsey the mistress of Samuel—and from these connections sprang the progeny which resembled Mr. Jefferson. Both the Henings girls were light-colored and decidedly good-looking. The Colonel said their connection with the Carrs was perfectly notorious at Monticello and scarcely disguised by the latter—never disavowed by them. Samuel's proceedings were particularly open. . . .

Colonel Randolph said that a visitor at Monticello dropped a newspaper from his pocket or accidentally left it. After he was gone he (Colonel Randolph) opened the paper and found some very insulting remarks about Mr. Jefferson's mulatto children. . . . Peter and Samuel Carr were lying not far off under a shade tree. He took the paper and put it in Peter's hands, pointing to the article. Peter read it, tears coursing down his cheeks, and then handed it to Samuel. Samuel also shed tears. Peter exclaimed, "Ar'nt you and I are couple of———pretty fellows to bring this disgrace on poor old uncle who has always fed us! We ought to be———by———! . . ."

Do you ask why I did not state, at least hint the above facts in my life of Jefferson? I wanted to do so, but Colonel Randolph, in this solitary case alone, prohibited me from using at my discretion the information he furnished me with. When I rather pressed him on the point, he said, pointing to the family graveyard, "You are not bound to prove a negation. If I should allow you to take Peter Carr's corpse into Court and plead guilty over it to shelter Mr. Jefferson, I should not dare again to walk by his grave: he would rise and spurn me." I am exceedingly glad Colonel Randolph did overrule me in this particular. I should have made a *shameful* mistake. If I had *unnecessarily* defended him (and it was purely *un*necessary to offer any defense) at the expense of a dear nephew—and a noble man—hating(?) a single folly. . . .

I write this *currente calamo*, and you will not understand that in telling what Colonel Randolph and others said, I claim to give their precise language. I give it as I now recall it. I believe I hit at least the essential purport and spirit of it in every case.

Parton, in his life of Jefferson, published in 1874, gave the substance of the above conversation between Randolph and Randall without using the full text.[2]

Referring to the quotation from Randolph concerning his unwillingness to allow Randall "to take Peter Carr's corpse into Court . . . to shelter Mr. Jefferson," Mrs. Brodie provides us with the following astonishing comment: "So the grandson by unconscious innuendo suggested the truth of that which he had just vehemently denied."[3] This "unconscious innuendo" is, we fear, too subtle for most ordinary mortals to grasp.

Randolph did make some statements to Randall that were obviously incorrect, if Randall quoted him accurately. He said he "had charge at Monticello" during the period when Sally was having her children, and he knew, therefore, that his grandfather was innocent. Randolph was born in 1792 and did not begin to take charge at Monticello, to aid Jefferson, until 1814. He was only a boy during the years when Sally was having her brood—her last child was born in 1808. Randolph's claim to have "slept within sound of his [Jefferson's] breathing at night" also is highly questionable.[4]

It is difficult, however, to dismiss Randolph's circumstantial account of the two nephews' reaction to the newspaper article. This episode is recounted in too much detail for Randall to have been mistaken as to its main outlines. Furthermore, it is altogether incredible that Randolph would have manufactured this out of the whole cloth, implicating his near relatives and putting words into their mouths, if they had not uttered them. He could have defended his grandfather without dragging in the Carr boys and having them confess their guilt.

And there is confirmation from two other sources. Ellen Randolph Coolidge, Jefferson's granddaughter, wrote her husband, Joseph Coolidge, Jr., in 1858 a long letter dealing with the "yellow children" at Monticello.[5] She said that "Dusky Sally" was "pretty notoriously the mistress of a married man, a near relative of Mr. Jefferson's, and there can be small question that her children were his. They were all set free at my grandfather's death, or had been suffered to absent themselves permanently before he died."

Later in the letter she decided that she might as well identify the "married man" in question, for she went on: "I will tell you in confidence what Jefferson [Thomas Jefferson Randolph] told me under the like condition. Mr. Southall and himself being young men together, heard Peter Carr say, with a laugh, that 'the old gentleman had to bear the blame for his and Sam's (Col. Carr) misdeeds.' There is a general impression that the four children of Sally Hemings were *all* the children of Col. Carr, the most notorious good-natured Turk that ever was master of a black seraglio kept at other men's expense. His deeds were as well known as his name."

Again, it seems reasonable to ask whether the granddaughter of Thomas Jefferson would have quoted one of her close relatives as accepting blame for the mulattoes at Monticello, and accused that man's brother of fathering Sally's children, if she had not been confident that she was speaking the truth. Like her brother, Thomas J. Randolph, she was naturally anxious to clear her grandfather's name, but she did not have to implicate her cousins in the process.

Ellen Coolidge went on to say that the reported immoralities of Thomas Jefferson "were never suspected by his own family—that his daughter and her children rejected with horror and contempt the charges brought against him. . . . His apartments had no private entrance not perfectly accessible and visible to all the household." She then observed, "I would put it to any fair mind to decide if a man so admirable in his domestic character as Mr. Jefferson, so devoted to his daughters and their children, so fond of their society, so tender, considerate, refined in his intercourse with them, so watchful over them in all respects, would be likely to rear a race of half-breeds under their eyes and carry on his low amours in the circle of his family."

As John C. Miller writes in *The Wolf By the Ears* (page 170), "the only question in the minds of those who lived at Monticello was whether Peter or Samuel Carr was the father of Sally Hemings's children."

The third important bit of evidence in behalf of Jefferson's innocence comes from Edmund Bacon, the longtime overseer at Monticello. In 1862, many years after Jefferson's death, when Bacon had moved to Kentucky and become a prosperous planter and horse-breeder, he was interviewed by the Reverend Hamilton W. Pierson, president of Cumberland College, Princeton, Kentucky. Pierson spent several weeks with Bacon taking down his recollections concerning Jefferson and Monticello. Pierson spoke of Bacon as "a man of wealth and character." When Bacon left Monticello in 1820 for good, Jefferson gave him a reference terming him "an honest, correct man in his conduct and worthy of confidence." Thomas Mann Randolph, Jr. gave him a similar reference.[6]

Bacon told Pierson about Sally's daughter Harriet, saying:

He [Jefferson] freed one girl some years before he died, and there was a great deal of talk about it. She was nearly as white as anybody, and very beautiful. People said he freed her because she was his own daughter. She was not his daughter; she was ———'s daughter. I know that. I have seen him come out of her mother's room many a morning when I went up to Monticello very early. When she was nearly grown, by Mr. Jefferson's direction, I paid her stage fare to Philadelphia and gave her $50. I have never seen her since and don't know what became of her. From the time she was large enough, she always worked in the cotton mill. She never did any hard work.[7]

The party who was seen coming out of Sally's room "many a morning" was evidently either Peter or Sam Carr; it certainly wasn't Jefferson. The name apparently was deleted by Pierson. The latter said in his Preface (page 6) that he would have omitted certain facts "in regard to the intemperance, and other vices . . . of some who were connected with Mr. Jefferson's family," had not a "distinguished historian" persuaded him to include them. However, he couldn't bring himself to publicize this particular name.

Since Jefferson had been dead for more than a third of a century when Bacon gave his interview, and Bacon was living in Kentucky, the latter was under no obligation or pressure to misrepresent what he had seen with his own eyes long before. The girl Harriet to whom he referred was falsely alleged to have been sold into a life of prostitution in New Orleans, but, as already noted, she married and settled in either Albemarle County, Virginia, or Washington, D.C. Bacon did err in one respect. He said the man he saw frequently emerging from Sally's room was Harriet's father. Quite probably he was, but Harriet was born in 1801, five years before Bacon was employed as overseer. The child born in 1808, two years after Bacon came to Monticello, was Eston, whom this same man doubtless fathered. The important fact, of course, is that Bacon saw the man coming out of Sally's room often in the early morning.

Mrs. Brodie's attempted refutation of the claim that Peter and Sam Carr, not Jefferson, were the guilty parties at Monticello, revolves around the fact that both had married and "were elsewhere, managing plantations with slaves of their own, during most of the years that Sally Hemings was bearing children at Monticello." This proves absolutely nothing. Both men had been married for a number of years when Bacon saw one of them emerging repeatedly from Sally's room. Sam—the more probable paramour of Sally—and his wife lived first a few miles away at Dunlora and then on the South Fork of the Rivanna River, also not far from Monticello.[8] It can be assumed that both nephews were frequent visitors on the mountaintop, along with Jefferson's other relatives.

But, says Mrs. Brodie, "no one has explained how either [Peter or Sam] could have fathered the eldest son, Tom, who had been conceived in Paris."[9] Half a dozen leading historians have concluded, for good reasons, that there was no such person as Tom, and that Sally was not pregnant when she returned from Paris. (See Chapter 4.)

Members of what Mrs. Brodie terms the "Jefferson Establishment," who seriously question whether there was a thirty-eight-year relationship between Jefferson and Sally, deny Jefferson "his capacity for love," she declared in the *Chicago Tribune* (July 3, 1979). A more irrelevant comment could hardly be imagined. Are we to understand that, in Mrs. Brodie's view, any widower who fails to take a mistress thereby proves himself incapable of loving?

Jefferson's unwillingness to contradict publicly the allegations that he had taken Sally as his concubine is readily explained by the fact that, in so doing, he would almost certainly have implicated other members of his family. Bear in

mind that his father-in-law, John Wayles, was widely regarded as the sire of Sally Hemings and five other children by
the slave Betty Hemings, and that these illegitimates were
therefore the half-sisters and brothers of Jefferson's beloved
wife. Consider also that his two nephews, Peter and Sam
Carr, were in all likelihood the progenitors of other groups of
mulattoes at Monticello, including Sally's children. In pro-
claiming his own innocence, Jefferson could hardly have
avoided implicating his close kin. He chose to suffer in silence.

7

His Family Never Wavered

If Thomas Jefferson was carrying on a thirty-eight-year affair with Sally Hemings at Monticello and begetting five mulattoes, one would hardly expect his lawful children and grandchildren to remain conspicuously loyal and affectionate throughout those years and thereafter. Yet no one who reads their letters to him, and about him, can doubt their unwavering devotion and respect. It is inconceivable, furthermore, that they could have been unaware of such a liaison, if it existed, especially in view of the manner in which the allegations concerning it were blazoned to the world in the hostile press. Jefferson, in addition, was alleged to have returned from France with Sally in an advanced state of pregnancy, along with his daughters, in 1789. The children and grandchildren of Thomas Jefferson were in a position to know whether this happened, and they obviously didn't believe it or any of the other charges hurled at their adored father and grandfather by Callender and those who parroted the allegations of that notorious liar and scandalmonger.

Jefferson wrote his children and grandchildren lovingly and often. His letters are not only tender but demanding, for he was anxious that they should grow up to be cultivated and accomplished men and women. Martha (Patsy) and Mary (Maria or Polly) were the only two of Jefferson's six children

83

who reached adulthood. Their mother died when they were young, and their father devoted much care and thought to their upbringing. Busy as he was with affairs of state, Jefferson usually found time to write them long and affectionate letters, inquiring as to their well-being and giving them instructions. These communications, it must be admitted, seem too solemn and moralistic when read today, and are so demanding as to be almost incredible. Consider, for example, his directive to eleven-year-old Patsy concerning the regimen of study that he expected her to pursue:

> With respect to the distribution of your time the following is what I should approve:
> from 8 to 10 o'clock practice music.
> from 10 to 1 dance one day and draw another.
> from 1 to 2 draw on the day you dance, and write a letter the next day.
> from 3 to 4 read French.
> from 4 to 5 exercise yourself in music.
> from 5 till bedtime read English, write & c.

Just when poor Patsy was to relax and enjoy herself is not clear. Apparently her father did not expect her to indulge in such aimless pursuits.

He concluded his letter with the following: "I have placed my happiness on seeing you good and accomplished; and no distress which this world can now bring on me would equal that of your disappointing my hopes. If you love me, then strive to be good under every situation . . . and [this] will go far towards ensuring you the warmest love of your affectionate father. . . ."[1]

Patsy was not alienated by these exacting admonitions—quite the contrary. She remained extremely close to her father throughout his life, both before and after her marriage. In fact she wrote him that no one, not even her husband, could ever replace him in her affections.

A not dissimilar, albeit less specific, communication went to Polly, then barely in her teens. Only the draft of this letter survives, but it is presumed to be identical, at least in substance, with the letter that was actually sent. The draft follows:

> I write you merely to tell you that I am well, and to repeat what I have so often before repeated, that I love you dearly, am always thinking of you, and place much of the happiness of my life in seeing you improved in knowledge, learned in all the domestic arts, useful to your friends and good to all. . . . Go on then, my dear Maria in your reading, in your attention to your music, in learning to manage the kitchen, the dairy, the garden and other appendages of the household, in suffering nothing to ruffle your temper or interrupt that good humor which is so easy and so important to render habitual, and be assured that your progress in these things are objects of constant prayer with yours affectionately. . . .[2]

Maria (or Polly), although considered decidedly better looking than Martha (Patsy), was shy and retiring, in contrast to her older sister. The latter was often in charge at Monticello, and for part of her father's second presidential term managed affairs at the White House. John Randolph of Roanoke termed Patsy "the noblest woman in Virginia," and Peachy R. Gilmer, a contemporary, said she was "the most accomplished woman in Virginia." Edmund Bacon, the Monticello overseer, declared that "few such women ever lived: I never saw her equal." Furthermore, she was "always in a happy mood." Isaac Jefferson, the former slave at Monticello, described Patsy as "a mighty peaceable woman; never holler for servant: make no fuss nor racket: pity she ever died." He went on that she was "tall like her father; Polly was low like her mother, and long ways the handsomest; pretty lady just like her mother." Patsy was easily the more talented of the two, and made by far the greater impact on the family circle. She married Thomas Mann Randolph, Jr., a future governor of Virginia, and they had twelve children, all but one of whom grew to adulthood. Randolph, who showed great promise, later become extremely erratic and a burden to his family.

As a letter-writer, Jefferson was astonishingly prolific. It has been estimated that he wrote and received as many as 50,000 letters. No fewer than 18,000 in his own hand survive. When he broke his wrist in Paris and had to write with his left hand, and much later when rheumatism and old age made writing slow and difficult, he nevertheless kept up his vast correspondence. Periodic headaches compounded the difficulties. In his final years he said that it took him almost an entire day to fill a single page. Jefferson wrote John Adams in 1822 that he counted up the number of letters he had received in 1820, and the total was 1,267, "many of them requiring answers of elaborate research, and all of them answered with due attention and consideration." He was always delighted to correspond with his children and grandchildren, no matter what the difficulty. In accord with the quaint custom of the day, he referred to Patsy's young husband in his letters as "Mr. Randolph," and to Polly's youthful spouse, John Wayles Eppes, as "Mr. Eppes." The girls wrote of their husbands in similarly formal terms.

Jefferson instructed his daughters to write him once a week, which they often failed to do, but their letters always showed much affection. He agreed to write them weekly also, and he too failed at times to live up to his side of the bargain. He reproved the girls for their shortcomings as correspondents, and they in turn chided him good-naturedly. On one occasion Polly called attention to the fact that they had not heard from him for six weeks.

There is little humor in the correspondence between Jefferson and Patsy and Polly. One of the few examples occurred in a letter from the youthful Patsy when the family

The polygraph, one of Jefferson's ingenious devices, by means of which he could copy any letter without extra effort. Some 18,000 letters in his own hand survive.

was in France. She wrote her father, "There was a gentleman, a few days ago, that killed himself because he thought his wife did not love him. They had been married ten years. I believe that if every husband in Paris was to do as much, there would be nothing but widows left."

In addition to devoting much time to the instruction of his daughters, Jefferson relished romping on the lawn at Monticello with their children, who called him "Grandpa." He was solicitous for the grandchildren's schooling, of course, and he offered to pay, despite his straitened circumstances, for the education of three of his grandsons, Lewis, Ben, and George Randolph. "I will send them to any schools you should prefer," he told their father, "and direct any course you may desire." The offer was accepted.[3]

Jefferson was crushed in 1804 when Polly died at age twenty-five. Her death, like that of his wife years before, was caused by complications following the birth of a daughter, who died a few months later. Polly's only surviving child was three-year-old Francis Eppes VII, who lived until 1881.

In his grief, Jefferson wrote his longtime friend, John Page, "Others may lose of their abundance, but I, of my want, have lost even the half of all I had. My evening prospects now hang on the slender thread of a single life." Patsy was the sole survivor of his six children, and he remarked sadly, "Perhaps I may be destined to see even this last cord of parental affection broken."

Mrs. Brodie cannot refrain from adding the comment: In saying that Maria "was half of all that I had," his statement "might be thought to be an explicit repudiation of his slave children." As usual, she assumes the existence of Jefferson's unproved and unprovable slave offspring. She also indulges in one of her far-fetched interpretations of his language. In a letter largely on political matters, written the day before Maria died, Jefferson ended by saying, "He alone who walks strict and upright, and who, in matters of opinion, will be contented that others should be as free as himself, and acquiesce when his opinion is fairly overruled, will attain his object in the end. . . ." Mrs. Brodie offers a characteristic comment: "In this moment of impending tragedy he was certainly reflecting on the 'man who walks strict and upright,' and in the succeeding days of inexpressible sorrow he may have even further divided his 'good passions' from his 'bad passions' and taken refuge in denial and rejection of the children conceived by his dark and secret mistress."[4] We have here another example of Mrs. Brodie's surmises as to what Jefferson "may have" thought, with no evidence whatever as to its correctness.

The slanders spread against Jefferson in the 1790s by the Federalists and in 1802 by Callender and others failed to shake the love and respect of Jefferson's daughters. Consider the following from Polly, under date of January 11, 1803, several months after Callender's calumnies were published:

> We arrived here [at Edgehill] safe yesterday after a most disastrous journey sufficiently distressing in itself but more so at the time from the depression of spirits felt on leaving you. The pain of seeing you turn back alone after having experienced so many happy hours with you, My dear Papa in the little room to us endear'd by your sitting in it always . . . made my heart ache I must confess in no slight degree. . . . How much do I think of you at the hours which we have been accustomed to be with you alone My dear Papa and how much pain it gives me to think of the unsafe and solitary manner in which you sleep upstairs. Adieu, dearest and most beloved of fathers. I feel my inability to express how much I love and revere you. But you are the first and dearest to my heart. . . .[5]

And Patsy wrote under date of May 31, 1804:

> No appology can be necessary for writing lengthily to me about yourself. I hope you are not yet to learn that no

subject on earth *is* or *ever can be* so dear and interesting to
me . . . I do not hesitate to declare if my other duties
could possibly interfere with my devotion to you I should
not feel a scruple in sacrificing them, to a sentiment
which has litterally "grown with my growth and
strengthened with my strength," and which no subsequent attachment has in the smallest degree weakened.
It is truly the happiness of my life to think that I can
dedicate the remainder of it to promote yours. It is a
subject, however, upon which I ought never to write for
no pen on earth can do justice to the feelings of my
heart. . . . Adieu, Dearly beloved Father. Believe me,
with a tenderness not to be expressed, yours most affec-
tionately. . . .[6]

The foregoing letters are typical of others over the years.
They demonstrate conclusively the devotion of Jefferson's
daughters and their complete confidence in his innocence of
the charges that were being published so widely.

But Mrs. Brodie comes up with the incomprehensible
statement that Martha "engaged in a heightened and almost
palpable seduction of her father in her letters, a seduction that
was as innocent as it was unconscious" (page 294).

If the reader finds this mystifying, to put it mildly, this is
hardly surprising. We herewith present the background, such
as it is, for Brodie's arrival at this rather staggering conclusion.

Brodie refers to Jefferson's "continuing intimacy" with
Sally Hemings and states that it had an effect that was "not as
irrecoverable as one might suppose." Jefferson was to be away
from Monticello on one occasion, and he told Maria that she
would be in charge during his absence. "Maria, however, had
responded with great delicacy" by saying, "The servants we
shall carry up will be more than sufficient for ourselves and
you would perhaps prefer yours to be employed in some way
or other." Mrs. Brodie adds that "No one could have lived

long at Monticello without knowing that Sally Hemings was in charge of Jefferson's 'chamber and wardrobe.' " Such was the statement of Madison Hemings, but even if this is correct, what does it prove? Brodie goes on to say, as though it had great significance, "Martha's own son related that his mother never sat in her father's bedroom-sitting room. It was, he wrote, Jefferson's *sanctum sanctorum.*" Is this supposed to be evidence that Sally sat or slept there? Brodie goes on: "Something of the nature of the accommodation Jefferson's daughters made is revealed in the nuances of their correspondence with their father. Two surprises emerge from their letters, one that Jefferson was in a continuing agony of apprehension lest he lose his daughters' love, and second, that Martha, at least, instead of showing revulsion and indignation, engaged in a heightened and almost palpable seduction of her father in her letters. . . ."

Jefferson's constant solicitude for his daughters and his obvious desire to retain their love is here termed, for some unknown reason, an "agony of apprehension." And Mrs. Brodie is clearly nonplussed by the fact that Martha shows "no revulsion or indignation," a fact that seems hardly astonishing, since Martha saw no grounds for showing any. Quite the contrary, as is abundantly evident from her correspondence with her father. As for her "seduction" of the latter, Mrs. Brodie may have known what this connotes, but does anyone else?

Webster's Unabridged Dictionary defines "seduction" as "act of seducing; enticement, esp. to wrongdoing, specif., the offense of inducing a woman to surrender her chastity . . . means of corrupting; now also, without evil implication, allurement; attraction; as, the *seductions* of wealth or art."

In what sense is the term being used to denote Martha's attitude toward her father? Mrs. Brodie is so obsessed with sexual matters that one supposes that her reference has Freudian implications, but what are they? How does one seduce one's father "in letters," and at the same time "innocently" and "unconsciously"? It boggles the imagination.

But let us continue. Mrs. Brodie finds sinister implications (page 295) in the fact that when Jefferson was inaugurated as vice-president at Philadelphia in 1797, he wrote Maria and her husband, but mentioned "not a single detail of the ceremony." However, there was "an almost desperate affirmation of affection," as follows: "On my part, my love to your sister and yourself knows no bounds, as I scarcely see any other object in life, so would I quit it with desire whenever continuance in it shall become useless to you." He "did not honor either of his daughters by real communication on any other level," says Brodie. On his return to his estate Jefferson wrote Martha, "The bloom of Monticello is chilled by my solitude. It makes me wish the more that you and your sister were here to enjoy it. I value the enjoiments of this life only in proportion as you participate them with me. All other attachments are weakening, and I approach the state of mind when nothing will hold me here but my love for yourself and your sister. . . ." Again, says Brodie, in a saturnine aside, "there was no description of the inauguration," but, she adds, "There was, however, an important communication, which Martha—the seducer and the seduced—could not have missed: *All other attachments are weakening; nothing will keep me in Monticello but my love for you and your sister.*" (Martha has now been metamorphosed into both "the seducer and the seduced," but this is probably as intelligible as was her previous incarnation, when she was merely doing the seducing.) Martha was worried over the inoculation of her children against smallpox, but she "nevertheless replied [to her father] immediately": "The anxiety I feel on their account my Dear Father does not prevent my feeling most sensibly for the solitude and gloom of your present situation. I never take a view of your solitary fire side but my heart swells. . . ." Isn't this a perfectly straightforward statement by Martha to her father that she is

Martha Jefferson Randolph, Jefferson's daughter, who often managed affairs at Monticello after her mother's death, highly praised for her ability and attractive personality. From a portrait by Thomas Sully.

depressed by the thought of his loneliness at Monticello? But under the penetrating eye of Mrs. Brodie this becomes something far different. She says, "Here we see an elaborate fiction being maintained between Jefferson and Martha concerning his relations with Sally Hemings. Martha would insist always that Jefferson's fireside was 'solitary' unless she was there to share it." One reason for such insistence could be that it happened to be based on fact.

Martha's sister Maria's letter to her father in 1803, quoted on a preceding page, is seen by Brodie, not surprisingly, as further evidence that there were diabolical goings-on at Monticello. Maria's reference to the "unsafe and solitary manner in which you sleep upstairs" signifies exactly the opposite, according to Brodie. Jefferson's daughter's deep affection, as expressed in the words "Adieu, dearest and most beloved of Fathers" brings Brodie's comment: "So the unconscious seduction back and forth continues" (page 365). Thus Maria has suddenly been involved by Brodie in the "seduction," along with Martha; not only that, it is "back and forth," whatever that may signify. "For this brief holiday Jefferson, it would seem, had had two adoring children," Brodie goes on, "with both husbands banished and both girls caught up in their father's orbit, with Black Sally and Mrs. Walker either explained, or ignored, or temporarily buried, and with Jefferson in any case forgiven." Such is psychobiography—or is it psychohistory?

Two of Jefferson's granddaughters, not to mention other grandchildren who did so, wrote of him with deep admiration and affection long after his death. They are Ellen R. Coolidge and Virginia J. Trist, children of Martha Jefferson Randolph.[7] In the 1850s, Mrs. Coolidge wrote Henry S. Randall, Jefferson's biographer, in part as follows:

> Our mother educated all her children to look up to her father, as she looked up to him herself—literally looked

up, as to one standing on an eminence of greatness and goodness. And it was no small proof of his real elevation that, as we grew older and were better able to judge for ourselves, we were more and more confirmed in the opinions we had formed. . . .

With regard to Mr. Jefferson's conduct and manners in his family . . . I can only repeat what I have said before . . . I have never known anywhere, under any circumstances, so good a domestic character as my grandfather Jefferson. I have the testimony of his sisters and his daughter that he was, in all the relations of private life, at all times, just what he was when I knew him. . . . As a child, girl and woman, I loved and honored him above all earthly beings. . . . My Bible came from him, my Shakspeare, my first writing-table, my first handsome writing-desk, my first Leghorn hat, my first silk dress. What, in short, of all my small treasures, did not come from him?

My sisters, according to their wants and tastes, were equally thought of, equally provided for. Our grandfather seemed to read our hearts, to see our invisible wishes, to be our good genius, to wave the fairy wand, to brighten our young lives by his goodness and his gifts. . . .

Virginia Trist wrote her reminiscences from France in 1839, in part, as follows:

These remembrances are precious to me, because they are of *him*, and because they restore him to me as he then was, when his cheerfulness and affection were the warm sun in which his family all basked and were invigorated. Cheerfulness, love, benevolence, wisdom, seemed to animate his whole form. . . . He would gather fruit for us, seek out the ripest figs, or bring down the cherries from on high above our heads with a long stick, at the end

Watercolor of Monticello in 1826, by an artist related to Thomas Jefferson, showing terrain where Jefferson played with his grandchildren as they gamboled and raced about the terraces and lawn.

of which there was a hook and a little net bag. . . . One of our earliest amusements was in running races on the terrace, or around the lawn. He placed us according to our ages, giving the youngest and smallest the start of all the others by some yards, and so on; and then he raised his arm high, with his white handkerchief in his hand, on which our eager eyes were fixed, and slowly counted three, at which number he dropped the handkerchief, and we started off to finish the race by returning to the starting-place and receiving our reward of dried fruit. . . .

Whenever an opportunity occurred, he sent us books; and he never saw a little story or piece of poetry in a newspaper, suited to our ages and tastes, that he did not preserve it and send it to us; and from him we learnt the habit of making these miscellaneous collections, by pasting in a little paper book made for the purpose any thing of the sort that we received from him or got otherwise.

On winter evenings, when it grew too dark to read, in the half hour which passed before candles came in, as we all sat round the fire, he taught us several childish games, and would play them with us. I remember that "Cross-questions" and "I love my Love with an A" were two I learned from him; and we would teach some of ours to him. . . .

Often he discovered, we knew not how, some cherished object of our desires, and the first intimation we had of his knowing the wish was its unexpected gratification. Sister Anne gave a silk dress to sister Ellen. Cornelia (then eight or ten years old), going upstairs, involuntarily expressed aloud some feelings which possessed her bosom on the occasion by saying, "I never had a silk dress in my life." The next day a silk dress came from Charlottesville to Cornelia, and (to make the rest of us equally happy) also a pair of pretty dresses for Mary and myself. . . .

The love and reverence felt for Jefferson by his children and grandchildren is abundantly attested in the foregoing quotations. Other similar statements have been omitted. These descendants were entirely aware of the mulattoes borne by Sally Hemings at Monticello, and of the charges that Jefferson was their father, but they were confident that the stories were false.

Mrs. Coolidge made the mistake of telling her sons that investigation proved Jefferson's absence from Monticello for fifteen months prior to the birth of one of Sally's children and that consequently he could not have been the father.[8] This is incorrect, for Jefferson was not only at Monticello nine months before the birth of that particular child, but it has been shown that he was on the premises nine months before each of the other births. While this proves nothing, it is unfortunate that Ellen Coolidge did not check her facts more carefully. She made this mistake when telling her sons that they should always defend the character of their great-grandfather.

This they did, and his other descendants followed suit. No group was more certain of Jefferson's innocence of these charges than those who were closest to him.

8

Jefferson and Slavery

From a flaming advocate in his younger days of slavery's abolition, Thomas Jefferson became less zealous in the cause during his later years. The reasons for this change of front have occupied the speculations of historians. Mrs. Brodie attributes his "political paralysis in regard to . . . emancipation" to his purported love affair with Sally Hemings.[1] Let us examine the validity of this assumption.

One of Jefferson's early attacks on slavery appeared in his *Notes on Virginia* (1782), where he wrote:

> The whole commerce between master and slave is a perpetual exercise of the most boisterous passions, the most unremitting despotism on the one part, and degrading submissions on the other. Our children see this and learn to imitate it. . . . The parent storms, the child looks on . . . gives a loose to his worst of passions, and thus nursed, educated, and daily exercised in tyranny, cannot but be stamped by it with odious peculiarities. The man must be a prodigy who can retain his manners and morals undepraved by such circumstances.

The paragraph Jefferson wrote for the Declaration of Independence concerning George III, which was eliminated as being too extreme, reads as follows:

He has waged cruel war against human nature itself, violating its most sacred rights of life & liberty in the persons of distant people who never offended him, captivating & carrying them into slavery in another hemisphere, or to incur miserable death in their transportation hither. This piratical warfare, the opprobrium of *infidel* powers, is the warfare of the *Christian* king of Great Britain, determined to keep open a market where MEN should be bought and sold. He has prostituted his negative for suppressing every legislative attempt to prohibit or to restrain this execrable commerce, and that this assemblage of horrors might want no fact of distinguished die, he is now exciting those very people to rise in arms among us, and to purchase that liberty of which *he* deprived them, by murdering the people on whom he also obtruded them; thus paying off former crimes committed against the *liberties* of one people, with crimes which he urged them to commit against the *lives* of another.

Also in his *Notes on Virginia* Jefferson wrote concerning slavery, "I tremble for my country when I reflect that God is just; that his justice cannot sleep forever." But he also declared much later, in 1821, "Nothing is more certainly written in the book of fate than that these people are to be free; nor is it less certain that the two races, equally free, cannot live in the same government."

This last was a view held by Jefferson throughout his career. While abhorring slavery, he felt that somehow the black and white races would have to be separated, with the blacks achieving a separate existence either in the unsettled western areas of the United States or in Africa, the Caribbean, or elsewhere. The American Colonization Society was formed in 1816 with a view to promoting the removal of free blacks to

Liberia. Jefferson not only favored this plan, but so did Abraham Lincoln several decades later.[2]

Jefferson was convinced that unless the process of emancipating and colonizing the blacks was got under way and carried through, the horrors of Santo Domingo, with its massacres of whites, would be visited upon this country. In a letter written in 1797 to St. George Tucker, another eminent emancipationist, Jefferson declared that, unless this were done, "we shall be the murderers of our own children." Such was his view to the end of his life.

In the hope of furthering this plan, the master of Monticello "recommended that black slave children be taken from their parents at the age of five, raised as wards of the states and prepared for their impending expatriation by instruction in skills that would prove useful to them in their new homeland."[3] Such a program seems highly inhumane today, and reminiscent of some Soviet or Asiatic dictatorship. But as John C. Miller points out, this plan "should be judged in the context of eighteenth century ideas." He declares that the Englishman John Locke, "sometimes apostrophized as the 'philosopher of the American Revolution,' proposed to put children of poor parents to work at three years of age, while Daniel Defoe reported with satisfaction that in Yorkshire most people above four years old appeared to be gainfully employed."

Jefferson believed that establishment of the emancipated slaves under a government of their own would be a "blessing for the blacks as well as the whites, since it would give them an opportunity to make a fresh start as a separate, free and independent people."[4]

Leonard W. Levy, an admirer of Jefferson but highly critical of him in certain respects, especially for his conduct during the trial of Aaron Burr and for his tactics in putting the embargo on foreign commerce, explains why he (Levy) did not

deal with Jefferson's attitude toward slavery in his book
Jefferson and Civil Liberties: The Darker Side: "I have . . . deliberately ignored the strain of racism in Jefferson's thought simply
because he cannot be held responsible for having been born a
white man in eighteenth century Virginia."[5]

The awkward position of Americans who owned slaves
during that period was noted by Dr. Samuel Johnson, who
asked, "How is it that we hear the loudest *yelps* for liberty
among the drivers of Negroes?"

By modern standards, Jefferson could perhaps be termed
a racist, but it is unfair to judge him on this basis. So eminent
a leader of the eighteenth-century Enlightenment as Benjamin
Franklin also might be termed a racist today, and that too
would be quite unfair. As a young man Franklin bought and
sold slaves in Philadelphia and made money in the process. He
also pronounced "almost every slave . . . by nature a thief."
Yet in 1758 Franklin proposed establishment of the first school
for Negroes in Philadelphia, and in 1787, near the end of his
life, he served as president of the regional abolition society.[6]

Pursuant to her thesis that Jefferson's infatuation for
Sally Hemings caused his zeal for emancipation to wither,
Mrs. Brodie accepts all the statements made by the aged
Madison Hemings in the *Pike County Republican* that do not
conflict with her assumptions.

She also accepts Madison Hemings's explanation of why
Sally did not remain in Paris indefinitely. Without giving any
authority for his assertions, Hemings declared, as quoted by
whoever wrote the interview, that his mother, then sixteen years
of age, refused to return to Virginia. "To induce her to
do so," he went on, "he [Jefferson] promised her extraordinary
privileges and made a solemn pledge that her children should
be freed at the age of twenty-one years. In consequence of his
promises, on which she implicitly relied, she returned with

him. . . . We all became free agreeably to the treaty entered into by our parents before we were born."[7]

About the only thing that is positively known concerning the foregoing alleged happenings is that Sally and James went back to Virginia with Jefferson and that Jefferson did free Sally's children. The notion that a sixteen-year-old slave would defy her master and seek to drive a hard bargain with him is incredible on its face. And there is no evidence that Sally was granted "extraordinary privileges" on her return; actually, there is every reason to believe that her position at Monticello was the same as that of the other house servants. Of course, Mrs. Brodie and Madison Hemings claim otherwise, and they also contend that Sally was pregnant by Jefferson when she crossed the Atlantic. There is no convincing evidence to support that theory either—quite the contrary.

Jefferson's uncompromising attack on the institution of slavery in his *Notes on Virginia*, mentioned above, was offset to some extent by other observations in that work—which, when written, was not intended for publication in the U.S. He said concerning Negroes:

> Comparing them by their faculties of memory, reason and imagination, it appears to me that in memory they are equal to the whites; in reason much inferior, as I think one could scarcely be found capable of tracing and comprehending the investigations of Euclid; and that in imagination they are dull, tasteless and anomalous. . . . Never yet could I find that a black had uttered a thought above the level of plain narration; never seen even an elementary trait of painting or sculpture. In music they are more generally gifted than the whites with accurate ears for tune and time, and they have been found capable of imagining a small catch.

Yet shortly thereafter Jefferson seemed to reverse himself, for he wrote, "the opinion that they are inferior in the faculties of reason and imagination must be hazarded with great diffidence." Furthermore, he offered the unprecedented proposal that blacks be educated at public expense, the males until age twenty-one and the females until eighteen. However, he added that they should then be transported out of the country, equipped with funds, seeds, tools and other necessities to enable them to establish themselves.[8]

When the Abbé Gregoire wrote him in 1809, praising various blacks for their accomplishments, Jefferson replied: "Be assured that no person living wishes more sincerely than I do, to see a complete refutation of the doubts I have myself entertained and expressed on the grade of understanding allotted to them [Negroes] by nature, and to find that in this respect they are on a par with ourselves. My doubts were the result of personal observation on the limited sphere of my own state . . . I express them, therefore, with great hesitation." While skeptical as to the achievements of Benjamin Banneker, black mathematician, and scornful concerning those of Phillis Wheatley, black poet, Jefferson subsequently wrote that he hesitated to declare the Negro inferior in mental capacity, since such a conclusion "would degrade a whole race of men from the rank in the scale of beings which their Creator may perhaps have given them."[9]

Jefferson was strongly opposed to the mixture of the white and black races, as is made clear on numerous occasions in his writings. (See Chapter 10.) By contrast, he favored the intermarriage of whites and Indians.

One characteristic statement on the former subject was made to Edward Coles, his neighbor in Albemarle County, Virginia. "The amalgamation of whites and blacks," Jefferson said, "produces a degradation to which no lover of his country, no lover of excellence in the human character, can innocently consent." While this statement should be clear to any reader, as John C. Miller declares in his important book *The Wolf By the Ears*, he thinks Brodie "strains credulity by piling implausibility upon implausibility." For she contends, he says, that "insertion of the word 'innocently' was deliberately contrived by Jefferson because he regarded himself as innocent of any wrongdoing with Sally Hemings; his love for her was undefiled by lust." Miller comments that "it is by the use of this kind of 'evidence' that she establishes her case for a romantic love affair between Jefferson and Sally Hemings."[10] (The title of Miller's book *The Wolf By the Ears* derives from Jefferson's statement in 1820 concerning the slavery issue: "We have the wolf by the ears: and we can neither hold him, nor safely let him go. Justice is in one scale, and self-preservation in the other.")

Jefferson's opinion of Indians was distinctly higher than his view of blacks. "We shall probably find that they [the Indians] are formed in mind as well as body, on the same module with the 'Homo sapiens Europaeus,' " he wrote. "In truth, the ultimate point of rest and happiness for them is to let our settlements and theirs meet and blend together, to intermix and become one people . . . and finally consolidate our whole country to one nation only."[11] The blacks were to be somehow removed.

Jefferson's ambivalence on the slavery question is illustrated further in his consenting reluctantly to the continuance of chattel servitude in the vast area acquired through the Louisiana Purchase, an acquisition that was perhaps the greatest achievement of his presidency.[12] His other major accomplishment was his leadership in abolishing the foreign slave trade by congressional act in 1808. One factor in his decision as to slavery's expansion into the Louisiana Purchase area was that he was the spokesman for the South, which was gradually losing its influence nationally. Then, too, much later, "when the Southern slaveholders met their first serious challenge in the Missouri contest, Jefferson was quick to see attacks on slavery as part of a diabolical conspiracy to weaken or destroy the Southern states," David Brion Davis writes in his *The Problem of Slavery in the Age of Revolution, 1770–1823* (pages 191–192).

In fairness to Jefferson, it should also be noted that in 1820 he wrote John Holmes: "Of one thing I am certain, that as the passage of slaves from one state to another would not make a slave of a single human being who would not be so without it, so their diffusion over a greater surface would make them individually happier, and proportionately facilitate the accomplishment of their emancipation, by dividing the burden on a greater number of coadjutors."[13]

Merrill Peterson says in his significant book *The Jefferson Image in the American Mind*, which won the Bancroft Prize:

> Jefferson was the crucial figure in American history both for slavery and for abolition. Partisans on both sides sought justification in him, while they also indicted him for their distresses. . . . How was it possible to reconcile the Jefferson of 1784 with the Jefferson of 1820? In 1784 he proposed to exclude slavery from the territories, and thus to stop expansion. In 1820 he denounced the Missouri Compromise restriction: "a fire-bell in the night" sounding "the knell of the Union." "There is a wonderful harmony and consistency in his life generally, and I would fain find it in this case, *if it exists*," Henry S. Randall [Jefferson's nineteenth-century biographer] wrote to Martin Van Buren. The consistency eluded Randall.[14]

Edmund Bacon, overseer at Monticello from 1806 to 1822, was high in praise of Jefferson's treatment of his slaves, and there is general agreement that this praise was justified. In an interview given in 1862, by which time Bacon had become a prosperous plantation owner in Kentucky, he said:

Mr. Jefferson was always very kind and indulgent to his servants. He would not allow them to be at all over-worked, and he would hardly ever allow one of them to be whipped. His orders to me were constant; that if there was any servant that could not be got along without the chastising that was customary, to dispose of him. He could not bear to have a servant whipped, no odds how much he deserved it.

Bacon also stated that the slave quarters at Monticello were not the customary cabins. "They were very comfortable, warm in the winter and cool in the summer," he declared. The "main, principal servant on the place" was Burwell. "Mr. Jefferson had the most perfect confidence in him," said Bacon. "He told me not to be at all particular with him—to let him do pretty much as he pleased."[15]

In his interview with the *Pike County Republican* in 1873 Madison Hemings said Jefferson "was uniformly kind to all about him." Isaac Jefferson, another slave at Monticello, interviewed in 1847 by Charles Campbell, a Virginia historian, termed Thomas Jefferson "a mighty good master" and "very kind to servants." "Mr. Jefferson . . . gave the boys in the nail-factory a pound of meat a week, a dozen herrings, a quart of molasses and a peck of meal. Give them that wukked the best a suit of red or blue, encouraged them mightily."[16]

Jefferson was considerate to his slaves, but he did not believe that the vast majority of them were sufficiently educated and trained to survive in a competitive world, unless they were given a substantial amount of additional instruction and furnished with the necessary tools, seed, and other supplies.

When Edward Coles told him in the early 1800s of his intention to sell his estate near Charlottesville and establish his slaves as free men and women on farms in Illinois, Jefferson

*Isaac Jefferson, a former slave at Monticello, who was interviewed in 1847
and whose likeness, above, was made at that time.*

tried to dissuade him. He wanted Coles to remain in Virginia and work for gradual emancipation there. Jefferson predicted that the freed slaves would fail as farmers because their lives under slavery had made them as "incapable as children of taking care of themselves."[17] He had expressed almost identical sentiments in a letter to Edward Bancroft in 1789, when he said, "As far as I can judge from the experiments which have been made, to give liberty to, or rather to abandon persons whose habits have been formed in slavery, is like abandoning children." Again, in 1811 he wrote John Lynch that it is "very certain that few of those advanced to a certain age in habits of slavery, would be capable of self-government." Indeed, he was convinced that "to emancipate one's Negroes would be a betrayal of duty, since only a few exceptional slaves could fend for themselves," David Brion Davis writes.[18] But Coles settled seventeen former slaves on tenant farms in Illinois near Edwardsville and gave them an opportunity to acquire ownership of 160-acre tracts on easy terms. "When Frances Wright visited Edwardsville in the 1820s, she reported that the liberated blacks spoke of their former master with tears of gratitude and affection," says John C. Miller. Coles was elected governor of Illinois in 1822 and was a leader in preventing the introduction of slavery there.[19]

Yet "it is possible . . . to credit Jefferson with effective anti-slavery leadership," David Brion Davis declares. He points out that William W. Freehling has pictured Jefferson as " 'the pragmatic statesman, practicing government as the art of the possible.' Professor Freehling faults the revisionists for taking a short rather than a long-run view of the question: 'What could be done—what Jefferson and his contemporaries did—was to attack slavery where it was weakest, thereby driving the institution south and vitiating its capacity to survive.' "[20]

Winthrop D. Jordan makes the point that Jefferson's failure to criticize slavery publicly in later years and to endorse the antislavery cause after his early militancy was due to "neither timidity nor concern for reputation." His caution arose from a fear that "premature endorsement by a figure of his prominence might easily damage the antislavery cause."[21]

"From the beginning," writes John C. Miller, "it was impressed upon Jefferson that he must choose between the preservation of his political 'usefulness' and active opposition to slavery."[22]

Advancing age may also have been a factor in Jefferson's increasing conservatism on the slavery question. In youth men often feel a burning desire to reform humanity and to correct evils which later in life appear less flagrant or less demanding.

One of the considerations that lessened Jefferson's zeal for emancipation must have been the huge financial sacrifice that would have been involved. The squire of Monticello was in financial straits; in fact, he was strapped during most of his public career. The pay in none of his numerous official positions did more than cover his expenses, and outlays during his diplomatic mission to France exceeded his salary. He was in public life from 1774 to 1809, except for the three years following 1793, and for one seven-year stretch he was not at Monticello at all. During these protracted absences the place was in the hands of overseers, some of whom were incompetent.[23]

A significant factor in bringing about Jefferson's fiscal stresses and strains, which in the end led to his insolvency, was the enormous cost of his forty-year remodeling of Monticello. Then there was his lavish hospitality, almost incredible in its dimensions. Fifty guests at a time, some of them uninvited, are known to have spent one night at the estate, and smaller numbers many nights. Numerous extra horse stalls were kept in readiness for such emergencies. Whole caravans of visitors, with their servants, descended on Jefferson over a period of many years, not to mention the members of his family who were in residence for long periods. The wine bill alone must have been formidable. As one example, a consignment of five hundred bottles arrived from Europe in 1793. In 1804 Jefferson ordered 400 bottles of champagne. He also was liberal in his outlays for books, which he often ordered in large quantities from England.[24] On top of all else, he endorsed a $20,000 note for his friend Wilson Cary Nicholas, United States senator and governor of Virginia. Nicholas became heavily involved in the depression of 1819 and then died, leaving Jefferson obligated for the money. Jefferson would have gone bankrupt in any event, but this was the *coup de grâce*.[25] In the end, following his death, Monticello and its contents had to be sold at auction, but the amount realized was insufficient to cover the obligations. Thomas Jefferson Randolph, Jefferson's grandson, paid the $40,000 deficit out of his own pocket.[26]

Since the number of slaves owned by Jefferson was in excess of two hundred at various periods, they constituted one of his principal assets. To have set them free would obviously have been a crushing financial blow.

Thus there were various reasons why the master of Monticello became less determined upon emancipation as the years went by. In addition to the overriding financial consideration affecting him personally, there was, on the national scene, the obvious problem of how to deal fairly with tens of thousands of illiterate and untrained free blacks who would suddenly be catapulted upon society. There were also the political implications of Jefferson's position as spokesman for the slave-holding South, with the possible jeopardizing of his influence through aggressive action. Hence it is clear that there were various plausible reasons for Jefferson's failure to press hard for emancipation. Mrs. Brodie's contention that this failure was due to his love for Sally Hemings simply does not stand up.

Jefferson never abandoned his conviction that slavery should somehow be eradicated. Less than a year before his death he declared that "the abolition of the evil is not impossible," and he added, "It ought never therefore to be despaired of. Every plan should be adopted, every experiment tried, which may do something toward the ultimate object."[27]

9

Those "Canonizers" of Jefferson

Jefferson's biographers who preceded Fawn Brodie have "canonized" him, she says in an article in the *Journal of Interdisciplinary History* (summer 1971, pages 155–171). "Where a biographer spends virtually a whole lifetime with a historical figure, as Dumas Malone has done with Thomas Jefferson . . . the involvement is total, and one may look for identification of major proportions," Mrs. Brodie declares.

She goes on to say that "this kind of canonization dominated nineteenth century biography, and there are striking examples even among highly respected American biographers of our own time. [Douglas] Freeman's multivolume lives of George Washington and Robert E. Lee are obvious examples." Even those biographers who are "wary of the impulse to sanctify are nevertheless often its victims," Mrs. Brodie declares; "they glorify and protect by nuance, by omission, by subtle repudiation, without being in the least aware of the strength of their internal commitment to canonization."

A quotation from Freud, one of her favorite authorities, is cited to buttress her thesis. Freud wrote that "biographers frequently select the hero as the object of study because for personal reasons of their own emotional life, they have a special affection for him from the very outset." He went on to assert that these writers then "devote themselves to a work of idealization, which strives to enroll the great man among their infantile models, and to relive through him, as it were, their infantile conceptions of the father . . . they thereby sacrifice the truth to illusion. . . ."[1]

The two Jefferson biographers who are singled out by Brodie for the charge of canonization are Dumas Malone and Merrill Peterson. She is high in praise of both men but sadly concludes that they are incapable of complete objectivity. Malone, she declares, "has come closer than anyone with his expert biographical brush," and is "a scholar's scholar." Peterson's *Thomas Jefferson and the New Nation* "takes the lead immediately among all rival biographies except for the work of Malone," and she speaks of Peterson's "brilliant monograph, *The Jefferson Image in the American Mind.*" Mrs. Brodie finds these books seriously flawed, nevertheless. Basically, what she is criticizing is the failure of both authors to accept the supposed liaison between Jefferson and Sally Hemings.

For she goes on to say: "Jefferson's biographers have been extremely protective of his inner life, or rather of his intimate life, which is not quite the same thing. There is important material in the documents which the biographers belittle; there is controversial material which they flatly regard as libelous, though it cries out for careful analysis. And there is what one may call psychological evidence which they often ignore or simply do not see."[2]

The foregoing was written several years before Mrs. Brodie published the biography of Jefferson she termed "an intimate history"; in it, as we have seen, she elaborated upon her view that all other biographers failed to grasp the nuances in the life of the man from Monticello. But her "careful analysis" often turns out to be unsound, and her "psychological evidence" tenuous in the extreme. And it is worth noting that Mrs. Brodie defends the relationship that she says Jefferson had with Sally, for she comments, "And there is no man to whose *character* it could be genuinely unbecoming. He [Jefferson] had been for years a widower." On another occasion she writes, "If the evidence should in the end point to its [i.e., Jefferson's relationship with Sally] authenticity [it] will turn out, under scrutiny, to represent not a tragic flaw in Jefferson but evidence of psychic health [and] not a flaw in the hero but in society."[3]

Mrs. Brodie speaks of what she calls the "Jefferson Establishment," the members of which, she says, are so protective of Jefferson that they cannot bring themselves to acknowledge his faults and frailties. "Certainly Charlottesville is the center of the Jefferson Establishment," she writes. "In addition to Malone and Peterson, the faculty includes Bernard Mayo, author of two volumes on Jefferson and a third, *Myths and Men*, which is dedicated to him, in part. A former bedroom on the second floor of nearby Monticello serves as the office of James A. Bear, Jr., director of the Thomas Jefferson Memorial Foundation, and editor, with the late Edwin M. Betts, of *The Family Letters of Thomas Jefferson* . . . Julian Boyd . . . resides . . . in Princeton . . . the only member of the Jefferson Establishment who lives outside the Charlottesville area...."[4]

One might conclude from the foregoing that these men are Virginians, dedicated almost from birth to the worship of Thomas Jefferson. As a matter of fact, only one of them, James Bear, is a Virginian, and he is also the only one who attended the University of Virginia. Malone—who, incidentally, regards George Washington as the greatest of all Americans—was born in Mississippi, Peterson in Kansas, the late Bernard Mayo in Maine, and the late Julian Boyd in South Carolina. Their college education was obtained at such institutions as Johns Hopkins, Harvard, Duke, and Yale, and those on the University of Virginia faculty served previously at such centers of learning as Princeton, Harvard, Brandeis, Yale, and Columbia. Furthermore, those living and working in and around Charlottesville were quite naturally attracted there by the superb collection of Jefferson materials in the university's Alderman Library and at Monticello.

None of the above-mentioned Jefferson scholars accepts Mrs. Brodie's thesis that Jefferson had a long-continued sexual relationship with Sally Hemings, or any such relationship at all. Other well-known historians who also do not accept her thesis are David Donald of Harvard, John Chester Miller of Stanford, and Harry V. Jaffa of Claremont College. These historians are united in the conviction that she has not proved her case.

Since, in Brodie's view, all members of the "Jefferson Establishment" canonize their hero and refuse to admit his faults, it is pertinent to examine some of their statements concerning Jefferson's more controversial activities and policies. In an interview with the Chicago *Tribune* (July 3, 1979), Mrs. Brodie was quoted as saying, "These men want to make an image of absolute perfection."

Let us scrutinize this "image of perfection," as pictured in the writings of Dumas Malone and Merrill Peterson, the two biographers whom Brodie regards as the "establishment's" principal "canonizers." President Jefferson's highly question-able conduct in connection with the trial of Aaron Burr for treason and in ramming the embargo legislation through Con-gress are selected for present purposes as offering golden opportunities for Malone and Peterson to demonstrate their overriding desire to depict a faultless paragon. Contrary to Mrs. Brodie's assertions, both men write scathingly of Jeffer-son's handling of these two situations.

Consider the statements of Malone concerning Jefferson's conduct before and during the Burr trial.

Before Burr had been tried, Jefferson, in a message to Congress, pronounced Burr "beyond question" guilty of treason. Malone terms this "most unfortunate" and an "irre-trievable blunder," as it certainly was.[5] He also wrote con-cerning Jefferson's attitude, ". . . his political enemies . . .

not improperly charged him with an original indifference which gave way to credulity, and with a measure of vindictiveness wholly inconsistent with his expressed convictions in regard to the sacred rights of the individual."[6]

"Jefferson cannot escape the charge of gullibility in his relations with [General James] Wilkinson," Malone continues. Wilkinson was termed by John Randolph of Roanoke "the most finished scoundrel that ever lived" and "the man whom the king [Jefferson] delighteth to honor." Malone observes that "this particular king was not at his best in dealing with scoundrels, especially this one." Jefferson "seemed to give his entire sanction to conduct which was regarded by many as arbitrary and tyrannical. Previously he himself had expressed disapproval of some of it in private," Malone says in reference to a defense Jefferson made of Wilkinson in a letter to him.[7]

And we have Peterson's assessment of Jefferson's conduct in this matter:

> Unfortunately Jefferson allowed himself to declare that Burr's guilt had been placed "beyond question." . . . Even Senator Plumer, for a long time an infidel on the subject, asserted, "There cannot now remain any doubt of Burr's seditious and treasonable designs—unless multitudes have conspired to establish falsehood." Old John Adams, in Quincy, doubtless agreed. "But if his guilt is as clear as the noonday sun," he remarked, "the first magistrate of the nation ought not to have pronounced it so before a jury had tried him."[8]

Peterson concurs with Jefferson's opinion that Burr was guilty, but is in complete disagreement with him as to the outcome of the trial, for he says:

> The verdict of common sense, of morality, and of history on Burr was, and must remain guilty. He might have

been convicted on a less stringent interpretation of the
treason clause, and but for [Chief Justice John] Marshall's
political bias this would surely have been the result. In
the long run, however, the nation was better served by
his bias than by Jefferson's. For conviction would have
introduced into American law the ancient English princi-
ple of "constructive treason," founded in the case on Burr's
"constructive presence" at Blennerhassett's Island, where
the evidence failed to pin overt acts of treason on him. It
was better that the scoundrel go free than be convicted on
evidence outside the indictment or on a constructive
definition of the act of "levying war." Jefferson could
hardly be expected to take this view of the matter.[9]

Let us now consider Malone's and Peterson's comments
on Jefferson's handling of the embargo, put into effect by
Congress, as a result of heavy pressure exerted by the president. The embargo prohibited United States vessels from
sailing to foreign ports and foreign vessels from taking on
cargo in American ports. President Jefferson saw the embargo
as the only alternative to war with Britain or subjection to
British demands. War came a few years later.

Malone writes: "The attempts to enforce the embargo
involved an exercise of arbitrary power by the Federal government and an inevitable and increasing infringement on
individual rights which were contrary to Jefferson's most
cherished ideals. . . . Forced to yield to a rebellious Congress
on March 1, 1809, he signed the Non-Intercourse Act, which
partially raised the embargo, and shortly afterward retired to
Albemarle, discredited and disillusioned, though unconvinced
that he had erred in policy."[10] Malone writes elsewhere that
"Jefferson's last months in office were anticlimactic, and he
was unimpressive during them."[11]

And Peterson has this to say: ". . . articles in the admin-
istration gazette explained the embargo better than anything

else published at the time. Yet they were not a substitute for a declaration by the president himself. . . . He betrayed his own principles of leadership, which underscored official openness and public trust, and contributed to the bewilderment and confusion surrounding the embargo." Later in the same book Peterson declares that "throwing the embargo into the hornet's nest on Capitol Hill was an act of supreme folly."[12]

So much for Mrs. Brodie's contention that Dumas Malone and Merrill Peterson desire to create in Jefferson an "image of absolute perfection." It seems hardly necessary to quote them further in refuting this assertion.

10

The Charge— Unproved and Unprovable

There are no anecdotes concerning Jefferson's alleged paramour, and she is not mentioned once in all the Jefferson correspondence. As John C. Miller puts it, ". . . we know virtually nothing of Sally Hemings, or her motives [and] she is hardly more than a name."[1] Yet there have been attempts to invest her with qualities and characteristics for which there is no evidence whatever. Page Smith, in his *Jefferson: A Revealing Biography*, pronounces Sally "intelligent, handsome, perhaps beautiful, full of spirit and fire, undoubtedly 'ardent'—a rewarding companion in bed" (page 208). Smith has no footnotes, and he provides us with no remote inkling as to where he could possibly have gotten such information. It goes beyond anything in Brodie, whose overall thesis as to the Jefferson-Hemings relationship he has accepted. There is nothing in Chase-Riboud's novel about Sally's "ardor in bed," and besides, that book appeared several years after Smith's.

The *New York Times Book Review* (June 15, 1980), announcing the appearance of the paperback edition of Chase-Riboud's *Sally Hemings*, refers to Sally as Jefferson's "beautiful, elegant, brainy, fiery and indestructible slave-companion." Presumably the reviewer was attempting to reflect the contents of the Chase-Riboud novel, without bothering to find out if this bit of "faction" gave an authentic

120

picture. The *Times* declared that the novelist "used facts that were ingeniously assembled by Fawn Brodie in her psychobiography of Thomas Jefferson." But there are no facts in Brodie's book to prove that Sally was "brainy" or "fiery," much less that she was Jefferson's "slave-companion." Furthermore, as we have seen, Chase-Riboud stated that "my Sally Hemings is not the historical Sally Hemings." So where did the *Times* get all this? We have here one more example of the manner in which myths concerning Sally Hemings have been accepted as truth and disseminated to countless readers.

Undismayed by the total rejection by the leading Jefferson scholars of her thesis as to the Jefferson-Hemings relationship, Brodie blandly reiterated and extended it in an article in *American Heritage* entitled "Thomas Jefferson's Unknown Grandchildren: A Study in Historical Silences."[2] In this article, published some two years after her Jefferson biography, she provided names and photographs of blacks in various parts of the United States whose claims to direct descent from Jefferson and Sally she unhesitatingly supported. She did reject the contentions of a group of Joe Fossett's descendants, on the ground that this craftsman in iron was the son of Mary Hemings and William Fossett, or Fosset, a white apprentice at Monticello. Brodie likewise did not accept the contentions of John Hemings's descendants that he was Jefferson's son.[3] But, as she puts it in her magazine article: "The stories of what happened to Jefferson's slave children and their descendants, long shrouded in mystery, are now emerging as a flood of information is being released by these long-silent heirs." This "flood of information" evidently consists of legends handed down in the various families concerned. "Since the publication of my *Thomas Jefferson: An Intimate History* (1974)," she writes, "descendants of Madison, Eston and Thomas have come forward with scrapbooks, family Bibles, private genealogies and pictures that have been quietly preserved over the generations. Their material is an exciting addition to the Jefferson family literature. . . . The black heirs had chosen to remain silent in the past because they were not believed. . . ."

There is nothing in Mrs. Brodie's article that provides any more proof that these individuals are descendants of Jefferson than she advanced in her biography. Much of her article is simply description of positions held by the persons in question in modern times, with photographs.

Mrs. Brodie again asserts as a fact that "Jefferson's liaison with Sally Hemings lasted thirty-eight years. . . . We know [sic] from a memoir written by Sally's third son, Madison, that she became pregnant by Jefferson in Paris in 1789. The son born shortly after the return to Monticello was called 'Tom' "—and so on and on, with the notorious Callender, Mrs. Brodie's "generally accurate reporter," given as the original authority and Brodie making futile efforts to prove that Tom actually existed. It is unnecessary to go again into a refutation of these confidently asserted "facts."

The magazine *Ebony*, published by blacks, in November 1954 carried an article entitled "Thomas Jefferson's Negro Grandchildren." Featured more prominently than any were the heirs of Joe Fossett, who, as noted above, was clearly not a Jefferson descendant. The claims of all the others also were almost certainly spurious.

Black historians, Mrs. Brodie has stated more than once, believe firmly that Sally was Jefferson's mistress, whatever may be the skepticism of many white historians. A notable exception among black historians is W. Edward Farrison, who concluded, after a comprehensive examination of the evidence, that it was impossible to be certain which side was right.[4]

Madison Hemings conceded that Jefferson showed no outward affection at any time toward him or Sally's other children. Hemings said in his interview with the *Pike County Republican* that the master of Monticello "was very undemonstrative" and "was not in the habit of showing partiality or fatherly affection to us black children. . . . He was affectionate toward his white grandchildren." Since Madison was born in 1805, he spent twenty-one years at Monticello during Jefferson's lifetime; yet he failed to mention one single expression of affection during that entire period toward himself or his brothers and sisters on the part of their "father." In the face of this, Mrs. Brodie would have us believe that there was a prolonged love affair between Jefferson and Sally which brought them several children and "much private happiness." Is it conceivable that a man of Jefferson's temperament, who showered affection and attention upon his white children and grandchildren to an almost excessive degree, would have ignored his "black children" by a woman with whom he was alleged to have been deeply in love for more than a third of a century? Nor did he provide opportunities for Sally's children to get any appreciable education, although he was constantly concerned with the schooling of the white members of his family. We have here additional grounds for believing that the black children at Monticello were not his.

Let us bear in mind also that Jefferson expressed extreme aversion to miscegenation many times over the years. In his *Notes on Virginia*, written during the American Revolution, he pointed out that Roman slaves were of the white race and went on to say (page 143), "Among the Romans, emancipation required but one effort. The slave, when made free, might mix with, without staining the blood of his master. But with us a second [effort] is necessary unknown to history. When freed, he is to be removed beyond the reach of mixture." Jefferson regarded miscegenation as "the horror of horrors," John C. Miller writes in *The Wolf by the Ears* (page 275). In a letter to William Short, dated January 18, 1826, only a few months before he died, Jefferson once more expressed his "aversion" to "the mixture of color in America."[5] It would indeed have been the height of hypocrisy for a man who entertained such views and expressed them over most of his adult life to have sired mulatto children.

In his *Man From Monticello*, Thomas J. Fleming says (page 282): "That Jefferson himself would have committed such an indiscretion [as fathering children by Sally]—and then recorded the results in his *Farm Book* in his own hand—at the very time when he was a committed candidate for the presidency, and continued the relationship through his two terms, when he was under the most relentless personal attack by the Federalists, is almost a refutation in itself. . . ."

In his *The Shackles of Power: Three Jeffersonian Decades* (page 155), John Dos Passos expresses agreement with Thomas J. Randolph's statement that one of the Carr brothers fathered Sally Hemings's brood. He declares that "defamatory stories" circulated against Jefferson became "part of the political mythology of the Jeffersonian era."

Harry V. Jaffa, of the Claremont College faculty, writes in the *Yale Alumni Magazine* (March 1980), in refutation of the allegations concerning Jefferson and Sally, "Madison Hemings had an interest in being known as the son of Thomas Jefferson, but there is no evidence—as yet known to scholars—to support the proposition that he was. . . . Today there seems to be an unbridled passion for stories debunking heroes, and if the stories are salacious, so much the better."

A number of reviewers of Fawn Brodie's Jefferson biography were highly complimentary, but there was not a Jefferson scholar among them. There were also caustic critiques, in addition to those quoted in earlier chapters.

The late Julian Boyd, editor of the massive *Papers of Thomas Jefferson*, whose encylopedic knowledge of Jefferson's career was universally recognized, made the following comment on the Brodie biography in a letter to friends:

> In the face of the unprovable and in confronting partial or contradictory evidence, the historian may and indeed

Jefferson in his old age, from a portrait painted by Thomas Sully at Monticello in 1821.

must employ inference, conjecture, and hypothesis. These are useful and legitimate tools of his craft. But the one thing he cannot do is to regard his own inferences and conjectures as proven facts. Yet this is what Mrs. Brodie has done throughout her volume and in respect to every aspect of Jefferson's life and character, the wholly conjectural account of his relations with Sally Hemings being only the most egregious example. . . . Even on the elementary level of verifiable fact her scholarship is lamentably deficient. Her *Jefferson* abounds in errors of detail. . . .

The great passion of Jefferson's life was directed toward the preservation of "the last best hope of earth," not toward a quadroon slave. He will survive and triumph over any ignoble Jefferson Mrs. Brodie may invent. But the real danger is that the methods of historical investigation she has employed may, if allowed to go unchallenged, begin to pass as intellectual coin of the realm.

Bruce Mazlish, professor of history at the Massachusetts Institute of Technology, wrote in the *Journal of American History* (May 1975) that "Jefferson was convinced that miscegenation meant 'degradation,' " and he asked, "Can readers believe that he would have conceived five children, one of them in the interval when he returned to Monticello for his daughter's funeral? . . . Brodie's analysis of the psychological situation is simply not convincing—which is not to say that her conclusion may not be right—though she there takes as bedrock what is still shifting sands of speculation."

The late Holman Hamilton, professor of history at the University of Kentucky, was almost lyrical in praise of Brodie's literary ability, but even he said, in the *Journal of Southern History* (February 1975) that "the closest thing to hard evidence in the book is limited to circumstantial evidence—

that Jefferson and Sally were in the same place when the children were conceived." He adds that "the volume's last chapter is entitled 'The Monticello Tragedy,' " but "the biographical tragedy is that the author chose not to eliminate a large number of dubious conclusions and worse. . . ."

"The 'intimate' of the title means mostly sex; all the usual Freudian jargon, interpretation, symbolism and so forth are evident," F. J. Gallagher wrote in his review for *Best Sell* (April 15, 1974). He went on to say that "the average reader who is seeking information on the career of Thomas Jefferson will find very little, while those seeking spicy gossip will, for the most part, find it rather boring after a few chapters."

"A fascinating and responsible book," said Alfred Kazin, the distinguished literary critic and author, in the *New York Times Book Review* (April 7, 1974), but "even after one reads all the evidence, one has the oddest disbelief about the whole story. It happened, yes, but to Thomas Jefferson?"

An almost ferocious attack was launched by Garry Wills of the Johns Hopkins humanities faculty in the *New York Review of Books* (April 18, 1974). "Two vast things each wondrous in itself combine to make this book a prodigy—the author's industry, and her ignorance," Wills wrote. "She has managed to write a long and complex study of Jefferson without displaying any acquaintance with eighteenth century plantation conditions, political thought, literary conventions, or scientific categories—all of which greatly concerned Jefferson. She constantly finds double meanings in colonial language, basing her argument on the present usage of key words. She often mistakes the first meaning of a word before assigning it an improbable second meaning, and an impossible third one."

Wills jeered at Brodie's seeking to read special significance into Jefferson's use of the word *mulatto* in describing the soil on a European tour, and added: "On the seven-week tour of Holland he used the word 'red' only seven times; but on the nine-week tour of Southern France he used it (or 'reddish') thirty-eight times. Such a disparity must reflect 'special preoccupation' of some sort, according to the Brodie method. Since his daughter had Jefferson's reddish hair and complexion, and he was arranging for her to come join him, the soil descriptions are really covert expressions of an incest drive. How on earth did Brodie miss this 'curious' fact?"

Wills was quoted further in the Washington *Post* (August 28, 1975) as saying, "I'm afraid that Professor Brodie, despite her admirable qualities, is the worst thing to happen to Jefferson since James Callender."

Yet, despite these scathing references, Wills somehow arrived in his review at the remarkable conclusion that Sally "was like a healthy, obliging prostitute" in her relations with Jefferson. "Her lot was improved, not harmed, by the liaison," he declared.

The Economist of London, reviewing the English edition, published by Eyre Methuen, said, in part (May 24, 1975):

> Her Jefferson is not the author of the Constitution of Virginia (three-quarters of a page) or of the Declaration of Independence (two pages), the Secretary of State (scattered references), the architect of the Louisiana Purchase (one paragraph) or even (his own proudest boast) the author of the Virginia Statute of Religious Freedom (one line). He is the would-be seducer of Betsey Walker (a chapter), the lover of Maria Cosway (another chapter), the father of five mulatto bastards by Sally Hemings, his slave girl (all or most of seven chapters, as well as an appendix). In this Mrs. Brodie has drawn freely on the panoply of psychoanalytical techniques made fashionable as "psychohistory" by Erik Erikson. . . .

The Economist concluded that the allegation against Jefferson was not proved when Callender published it, "and it has not been proved since."

Despite the vast overemphasis on sex in the Brodie opus and the skimpy treatment of Jefferson's enormous achievements in the realm of public affairs, John Barkham, the American critic, termed the book "the best-rounded single-volume biography [of Jefferson] I have yet read."

Under the heading "How Not to Write a Biography," Clifford Egan of the University of Houston history faculty, contributed a comprehensive essay review to the *Social Science Journal* (April, 1977). He said, in part:

> Looking at *Thomas Jefferson* two years after its publication, what is striking is that professional reviews were so gentle; the book suffers from serious flaws, defects noted by remarkably few reviewers. . . .
>
> Numerous cases of negligence with sources exist. . . . Brodie's *Jefferson* is riddled with contradictions. . . . When Brodie strays away from her speculation about Jefferson and the heart (the bulk of the book) and into Jefferson the public man, the result is sheer disaster as error follows error. . . . To Brodie's factual errors, contradictions and cavalier use of evidence must be added another sin—the injection of contemporary issues into evaluating the past. . . . *Thomas Jefferson* fails as biography and history. . . . Conventional scholars expect more than page after page of speculation in lieu of solidly documented material. . . .

Throughout her biography, Mrs. Brodie repeatedly refers to what she terms Jefferson's shame, suffering, and guilt. For example (page 32), she speaks of "a serious passion that brought Jefferson and the slave woman much private happiness. . . . It also brought suffering, shame, and even political

paralysis in regard to Jefferson's agitation for emancipation."
Brodie writes (page 297), "So the faint hint of apology, regret
and shame surfaced again." And on page 431: "That he
suffered from guilt there is ample evidence; it seems not to
have been a continuing, gnawing anxiety, but rather a tor-
menting surge of anguish when something specific forced
recognition upon him of the enormous difference between his
theoretical ideal society and his daily life." Furthermore (page
441), "The peace and serenity of Monticello was enforced by
Jefferson's remarkable will, by his capacity for ordering a
general happiness, by his denial of the suffering, the humiliation and the ugliness. . . . If the hatred and tyranny and
sadism of the whites would result, as he feared, in threatening
slave insurrection and a war of races, loving [Sally] brought no
real solution, only secrecy, denial, humiliation, guilt and
loss." And finally, "That he continued to suffer from anxiety
and guilt we see in the last letter of his life. . . ." (page 467).

Only a psychohistorian can find evidence of the all-
pervading sense of shame, suffering, humiliation, and guilt
that Mrs. Brodie has discovered in Thomas Jefferson. Her
entire thesis as to guilt is based, of course, on her assumption
that he had a secret relationship with Sally Hemings, something the leading authorities do not concede and for which she
gives no convincing evidence. Perhaps most astonishing is her
statement that this sense of guilt was present in the last letter
that Jefferson wrote, the famous communication of June 24,
1826, penned only ten days before his death. In this letter he
regretfully declined, because of illness, an invitation to speak
at the fiftieth anniversary celebration of the signing of the
Declaration of Independence. In ringing words he declared
that the Declaration "will be (to some parts sooner, to others
later, but finally to all), the signal of arousing men to burst the
chains under which monkish ignorance and superstition had
persuaded them to bind themselves, and to assume the bless-
ings and security of self-government." And then came the

celebrated passage: "All eyes were opened, or opening, to the rights of man. The general spread of the light of science has already laid open to view the palpable truth, that the mass of mankind has not been born with saddles on their backs, nor a favored few, booted and spurred, ready to ride them legitimately by the grace of God. These are grounds of hope for others. For ourselves, let the annual return of this day forever refresh our recollections of these rights, and an undiminished devotion to them."[6] These eloquent and stirring words are as far from evidencing a sense of guilt as could well be imagined.

Despite her constant references to Jefferson's shame, guilt, and humiliation, Mrs. Brodie protests (page 32) that his "heroic image remains untarnished." Mrs. Chase-Riboud, in one of her publisher's press releases, declares that "tragedy and secrecy, ambiguity and hypocrisy—all these elements combine in the story." Yet she too asserts that "in no way does Jefferson's romantic involvement with Sally Hemings detract from the grandeur of his genius or call into question his place in American history." Shame, guilt, and hypocrisy seem decidedly dubious ingredients for heroic images and exalted leadership in American history. It is impossible to reconcile the foregoing statements.

The three leading Jeffersonian authorities in the world, Malone, Peterson, and Boyd, have never been able to discover that Jefferson had anything remotely resembling a guilt complex. Julian Boyd spoke for all three of them when he repudiated completely Brodie's picture of a "despairing, ambivalent, indecisive, guilt-ridden man." He went on to say that "the principal defect of Brodie's work is the manipulation of evidence, the failure to give due weight to the overwhelming considerations of fact and plausibility which conflict with her preconceptions." Boyd added that Mrs. Brodie's Jefferson "never existed."

Malone, whose magisterial life of Jefferson was awarded the Pulitzer Prize, wrote apropos of Mrs. Brodie's biography:

"This determined woman carries psychological speculation to the point of absurdity. The resulting mishmash of fact and fiction, surmise and conjecture is not history as I understand the term. Mrs. Brodie is not without insight into Jefferson's personality, and except for her obsession, might have contributed to our understanding. But to me the man she describes in her more titillating passages is unrecognizable. She presents virtually no evidence that was not already known to scholars and wholly disregards testimony which I regard as more reliable."

Peterson, the greatly respected Jefferson scholar whose books are acknowledged by Mrs. Brodie to be of the highest quality, writes, "Mrs. Brodie has her obsessive theory, and she sends it tracking through the evidence, like a hound in pursuit of game . . . in the end nothing is cornered and we are as remote from the truth as when we began. . . . I see no need to charge off in defense of Jefferson's integrity when we have no solid grounds for doubting it." Peterson goes on to say that Callender's newspaper article of 1802 "without supporting evidence of any kind, is the principal source of the legend, and in all likelihood we would not be discussing it today but for him. . . . Callender's known character, his motives, his talent for libel—none of this damages his credibility for Mrs. Brodie."[7]

It has been charged, incorrectly, that those who deny Jefferson's liaison with Sally Hemings but admit his impropriety with Betsey Walker are racists, since they do not register indignation over the Betsey Walker affair, involving a white woman. But Jefferson admitted that he made improper advances to Betsey in his youth, "when young and single," whereas there is grave doubt that he formed any sort of irregular relationship with Sally. Historians wish first to ascertain the truth of this latter allegation against one of the greatest Americans. Furthermore, Mrs. Brodie charges that

Jefferson had a guilt complex because of Sally, which she terms "the unwritten and unadmitted tragedy in Jefferson's life."[8] Leading Jeffersonians deny that any such complex or "tragedy" existed.

Compared with Thomas Jefferson's spectacular and fearless role in establishing American independence and the democratic institutions that we know today, questions concerning his relations with one of his slaves, though decidedly disturbing, are of relatively minor importance. Yet much has been made of these relations in recent years, and it is necessary that the facts become known, insofar as they can be ascertained.

Of greater, and indeed epoch-making significance are Jefferson's contributions to posterity in the realms of political democracy and intellectual and religious freedom. When he penned those deathless words, "I have sworn upon the altar of God eternal hostility against every form of tyranny over the mind of man," he summed up his philosophy and his impassioned faith. The lack of a Bill of Rights in the United States Constitution when it was adopted in 1788 was immediately noted by Jefferson, and he wrote at once from France, pressing for such an expansion of the new nation's organic law. All our civil liberties today are based on those amendments to the Constitution. In addition to his incomparable contributions in these areas, Jefferson's prodigious versatility made it possible for him to provide others of far-reaching significance in such fields as architecture, education, science, agriculture, and law. On top of all else, he was an accomplished musician, bibliophile, and philologist. No serious historian claims that Thomas Jefferson was without faults, but this philosopher-statesman is universally acknowledged to have been one of the most brilliant ornaments of the Enlightenment, an age that produced in America a group of men whose political genius astounded the world.

In the grave at Monticello lie the bones of one whose fame is secure, no matter what slanderous falsehoods were spread against him long ago by a disappointed and unscrupulous office-seeker burning for revenge.

Monticello as it appears today, visited by many thousands of tourists from all over the world. The west front is shown.

Notes

CHAPTER 1
INTRODUCTION

1. See John Halperin, "*Eminent Victorians* and History," *Virginia Quarterly Review*, Vol. LVI, No. 3 (Summer 1980), pp. 433–454.

CHAPTER 2
HOW IT ALL BEGAN

1. For Jefferson's payments to Callender (totaling almost $200), see Henry S. Randall, *The Life of Thomas Jefferson*, Vol. III, p. 18n.

2. Jefferson to Callender, October 6, 1799. Quoted by Charles A. Jellison in *Virginia Magazine of History and Biography*, Vol. LXVII, No. 3 (July 1959), p. 299.

3. *Ibid.*, p. 303.

4. Dumas Malone, *Jefferson and His Time*, Vol. I, pp. 447–451.

5. John C. Miller, *The Wolf by the Ears*, p. 154.

6. Douglass Adair, *Fame and the Founding Fathers*, p. 164n.

7. *Richmond Examiner*, July 27, 1803.

8. James Truslow Adams, *The Living Jefferson*, p. 315.

9. W. Edward Farrison, "The Origin of Brown's *Clotel*," Phylon, Vol. XV (1954), pp. 347–354.

10. *The Collected Works of Abraham Lincoln*, Roy P. Basler, editor, Vol. IV, pp. 111, 112n.

11. William Wells Brown, *Clotelle*, p. vii.

12. *Pike County Republican*, March 13, 1873.

13. Pearl M. Graham, "Thomas Jefferson and Sally Hemings," *Journal of Negro History*, Vol. XLVI, No. 2 (April 1961), pp. 89–103.

CHAPTER 3

THE HEMINGSES OF MONTICELLO

1. Abigail Adams to Jefferson, *Papers of Thomas Jefferson*, Julian Boyd, editor, Vol. XI, p. 503.
2. James A. Bear, Jr., "The Hemings Family of Monticello," *Virginia Cavalcade*, Vol. XXIX, No. 2 (Autumn 1979), p. 85.
3. Bear, *ibid.*, pp. 80–81.
4. *Ibid.*, p. 82.
5. *Ibid.*, pp. 82–84.
6. *Ibid.*, p. 87.
7. Fawn M. Brodie, *Thomas Jefferson: An Intimate History*, pp. 466–467.

CHAPTER 4

CALLENDER, COSWAY, AND SALLY

1. Fawn M. Brodie, *American Heritage*, Vol. XXVII, October 1976, p. 29.
2. John C. Miller, *The Wolf by the Ears*, pp. 153–154.
3. Dumas Malone, *Jefferson and His Time*, Vol. I, p. 396.
4. Carleton S. Smith in Preface to Helen D. Bullock's *My Head and My Heart*, p. ix.
5. Brodie, *Journal of Interdisciplinary History*, Vol. II, p. 162.
6. Malone, *op. cit.*, Vol. II, p. 76.
7. Charles B. van Pelt, *American Heritage*, Vol. XXII, No. 5 (August 1971), pp. 22–29.
8. Brodie, *Thomas Jefferson: An Intimate History*, pp. 223, 225.
9. *Pike County Republican*, March 13, 1873.
10. Brodie, *op. cit.*, p. 83.
11. *Pike County Republican*, March 13, 1873. Malone and Hochman, *Journal of Southern History*, November 1975, pp. 523–528.
12. Brodie, *op. cit.*, p. 292.
13. Brodie, *American Heritage*, Vol. XXVII, October 1976, pp. 98–99.
14. Miller, *op. cit.*, p. 156. Wills, *New York Review of Books*, April 18, 1974. Jordan, *White Over Black*, p. 466n. Peterson, letter to the author.

15. Brodie, *Thomas Jefferson: An Intimate History*, p. 438.

16. "General Lafayette's Visit," *Virginia University Magazine*, Vol. IV (1859), p. 125.

17. Brodie, *op. cit.*, pp. 229–230.

18. *Ibid.*, p. 230.

19. *Ibid.*, pp. 231–232.

20. Malone, *op. cit.*, Vol. IV, p. 433.

21. Brodie, *op. cit.*, pp. 232–233.

22. See "The Hemings Family at Monticello," *Virginia Cavalcade*, Vol. XXLX, No. 2 (Autumn 1979), p. 85.

23. Julian P. Boyd, editor, *Papers of Thomas Jefferson*, Vol. XIV, p. 426.

24. David Herbert Donald, "By Sex Obsessed," Vol. LVIII, No. 1 (July 1974), pp. 96–98.

25. Brodie, *op. cit.*, p. 222.

26. Brodie, *op. cit.*, p. 277.

27. See Boyd, *op. cit.*, Vol. XV, pp. 392–397.

28. Brodie, *op. cit.*, pp. 371–372.

CHAPTER 5

FICTION MASQUERADING AS FACT

1. As reported by Bill McKelway, *Richmond Times-Dispatch*, February 11, 1979.

2. Malone, *Jefferson and His Time*, Vol. IV, Appendix II, pp. 494–495.

3. Peterson, *Thomas Jefferson and the New Nation*, p. 707.

4. Brodie, *Thomas Jefferson: An Intimate History*, pp. 374–375, 543n.

5. Jackson's book was sponsored by the American Historical Association and published by Appleton-Century (New York) in 1942. See pp. 109–110.

6. Ellen R. Coolidge to Joseph Coolidge, Jr., October 24, 1858, as reported in the *New York Times*, May 18, 1974.

7. Thomas Jefferson to Martha J. Randolph, November 4, 1815, Betts and Bear, *The Family Letters of Thomas Jefferson*, pp. 411, 412. Bear, letters to the author, used by permission.

CHAPTER 6

ENTER THE CARR BROTHERS

1. Full text of letter in Milton E. Flower, *James Parton, the Father of Modern Biography*, pp. 236–239. Also in Brodie, *Thomas Jefferson: An Intimate History*, Appendix III, pp. 494–497.

2. See Parton, *Life of Jefferson*, pp. 569–570.

3. Brodie, *Thomas Jefferson: An Intimate History*, p. 440.

4. See Sarah N. Randolph, *The Domestic Life of Thomas Jefferson*, p. 376. See also Hamilton W. Pierson *Jefferson at Monticello*, p. 137n., —both reproduced in *Jefferson at Monticello*, James A. Bear, Jr., editor. See also *Farm Book*, p. 130.

5. Full text in the *New York Times*, May 18, 1974.

6. As reported by Pierson in Bear, *op. cit.*, pp. 34–36.

7. *Ibid.*, p. 102.

8. Brodie, *op. cit.*, pp. 493–494.

9. Brodie, *American Heritage*, Vol. XXVII, No. 6 (October 1976), p. 32.

CHAPTER 7

HIS FAMILY NEVER WAVERED

1. *The Family Letters of Thomas Jefferson*, Edwin Betts and James A. Bear, Jr., editors, p. 19.

2. *Ibid.*, p. 83.

3. *Ibid.*, pp. 11–12.

4. Fawn M. Brodie, *Thomas Jefferson: An Intimate History*, pp. 380, 381.

5. Betts and Bear, editors, *op. cit.*, p. 240.

6. *Ibid.*, p. 260.

7. See Sarah N. Randolph, *The Domestic Life of Thomas Jefferson*, pp. 291–298.

8. See Milton E. Flower, *James Parton: The Father of Modern Biography*, Appendix IV, p. 237.

CHAPTER 8

JEFFERSON AND SLAVERY

1. Fawn M. Brodie, *Thomas Jefferson: An Intimate History*, p. 32.
2. See Carl Sandburg, *Abraham Lincoln: The Prairie Years*, Vol. I, p. 449.
3. See John C. Miller, *The Wolf by the Ears*, pp. 270–271.
4. *Ibid.*, p. 272.
5. Leonard W. Levy, *Jefferson and Civil Liberties: The Darker Side*, p. xi.
6. Carl van Doren, *Benjamin Franklin*, pp. 129, 216, 774.
7. *Pike County Republican*, March 13, 1873.
8. *Notes on the State of Virginia*, pp. 137–139, 140, 143.
9. See Winthrop D. Jordan, *White Over Black*, pp. 437, 453, 455.
10. Miller, *op. cit.*, p. 207, 207n.
11. See Winthrop D. Jordan, *The White Man's Burden*, pp. 191–192.
12. Miller, *op. cit.*, pp. 142–145, 209.
13. *Works of Thomas Jefferson*, edited by Paul Leicester Ford, Vol. XII, p. 159.
14. Merrill D. Peterson, *The Jefferson Image in the American Mind*, pp. 188–189.
15. See Reverend Hamilton W. Pierson in *Jefferson at Monticello: The Private Life of Thomas Jefferson*, James A. Bear, Jr., editor, pp. 46, 97, 99.
16. "Memoirs of a Monticello Slave," as dictated to Charles Campbell by Isaac, in *Jefferson at Monticello*, Bear, editor, pp. 23, 36–37.
17. Quoted by Miller, *op. cit.*, p. 206.
18. David B. Davis, *The Problem of Slavery in the Age of Revolution*, p. 212.
19. Miller, *op. cit.*, pp. 207–208.
20. Davis, *op. cit.*, p. 168.
21. Jordan, *op. cit.*, p. 435.
22. Miller, *op. cit.*, p. 279.
23. See Sarah N. Randolph, *The Domestic Life of Thomas Jefferson*, pp. 342–343.

24. See Nathan Schachner, *Thomas Jefferson*, pp. 78, 95, 223; *The Family Letters of Thomas Jefferson*, Edwin M. Betts and James A. Bear, Jr., editors; p. 123; Paul Wilstach, "Jefferson's Little Mountain," *National Geographic*, April 1929, p. 500.

25. See Sarah N. Randolph, *op. cit.*, p. 351n.

26. See sketch of Thomas J. Randolph by Thomas P. Abernethy in *Dictionary of American Biography*, p. 370.

27. Quoted in Miller, *op. cit.*, p. 276.

CHAPTER 9

THOSE "CANONIZERS" OF JEFFERSON

1. Fawn M. Brodie, "Jefferson's Biographers and the Psychology of Canonization," *Journal of Interdisciplinary History*, Vol. II, Summer 1971, pp. 155–156.

2. *Ibid.*, pp. 156, 158, 161.

3. *Ibid.*, p. 170.

4. *Ibid.*, p. 157.

5. Dumas Malone, *Jefferson and His Time*, Vol. V, pp. 265, 342.

6. Malone, "Thomas Jefferson," *Dictionary of American Biography*, Vol. V, Part 2, p. 30.

7. Malone, *Jefferson and His Time*, Vol. V, pp. 276, 327–328.

8. Merrill D. Peterson, *Thomas Jefferson and the New Nation*, pp. 852–853.

9. *Ibid.*, p. 873.

10. Malone, *Dictionary of American Biography*, Vol. V, Part 2, p. 31.

11. Malone, *Jefferson and His Time*, Vol. V, p. xxiii.

12. Peterson, *op. cit.*, pp. 886, 911.

CHAPTER 10

THE CHARGE—
UNPROVED AND UNPROVABLE

1. John C. Miller, *The Wolf by the Ears*, p. 175.

2. *American Heritage*, Vol. XXVII, No. 6 (October 1976), pp. 28–33.

3. Fawn M. Brodie, *Thomas Jefferson: An Intimate History*, pp. 550–551 (n. 47) and 554 (n.45).

4. W. Edward Farrison, *C.L.A. Journal*, Vol. XVII, No. 2 (December 1973), p. 174.

5. *Works of Jefferson*, Paul Leicester Ford, editor, Vol. XII, p. 434.

6. Jefferson to Roger C. Weightman, June 24, 1826. See *Writings of Thomas Jefferson*, Lipscomb and Bergh, editors, pp. 181–182.

7. These quotations from Boyd, Malone, and Peterson are from letters to the author and used with their permission.

8. Brodie, *op. cit.*, p. 467.

Bibliography

Adair, Douglass. *Fame and the Founding Fathers*, Chapter VIII, "The Jefferson Scandals," New York: W. W. Norton, 1974. Published for Institute of Early American History and Culture, Williamsburg, Virginia.

Bailyn, Bernard. "Boyd's Jefferson: Notes for a Sketch." *New England Quarterly*, Vol. XXXIII (1960), pp. 380–400.

Basler, Roy P., editor. *Collected Works of Abraham Lincoln*, Vol. IV. New Brunswick: Rutgers University Press, 1953.

Bear, James A., Jr., editor. *Jefferson at Monticello*, including "Memoirs of a Monticello Slave," as dictated to Charles Campbell by Isaac; and *Jefferson at Monticello: The Private Life of Thomas Jefferson* by Reverend Hamilton W. Pierson (Introduction by James A. Bear, Jr.). Charlottesville: University of Virginia Press, 1967.

Bear, James A., Jr. "The Hemings Family at Monticello." *Virginia Cavalcade*, Vol. XXLX, No. 2 (Autumn 1979), pp. 78–87.

Becker, Carl L. *The Declaration of Independence*. New York: Alfred A. Knopf, 1966.

Betts, Edwin M. *Thomas Jefferson's Farm Book*. Princeton: Princeton University Press, 1953. Published for American Philosophical Society.

——— and Bear, James A., Jr. *The Family Letters of Thomas Jefferson*. Columbia, Mo.: University of Missouri Press, 1966.

Boyd, Julian P., editor. *The Papers of Thomas Jefferson* (19 volumes). Princeton: Princeton University Press, 1950–1974.

Brodie, Fawn M. "The Political Hero in America." *Virginia Quarterly Review*, Vol. XL, No. 1 (Winter 1970), pp. 46–60.

―――. "Jefferson's Biographers and the Psychology of Canonization." *Journal of Interdisciplinary History*, Vol. II, Summer 1971, pp. 155–171.

―――. "The Great American Taboo." *American Heritage*, Vol. XXIII, No. 4 (June 1972), pp. 48–57.

―――. *Thomas Jefferson: An Intimate History*. New York: W. W. Norton, 1974.

―――. "Thomas Jefferson's Unknown Grandchildren: A Study in Historical Silences." *American Heritage*, Vol. XXVII, No. 6 (October 1976), pp. 28–33, 94–99.

Brown, William Wells. *Clotelle: A Tale of the Southern States*. Reprint Edition. Philadelphia: Albert Saifer, 1955.

Bruckberger, R. L. *Image of America*. New York: Viking Press, 1959.

Bullock, Helen Duprey. *My Head and My Heart*. New York: G. P. Putnam's Sons, 1945.

Callender, James T. The Prospect Before Us (3 volumes). Richmond: 1800, 1801.

Chase-Riboud, Barbara. *Sally Hemings*. New York: Viking Press, 1979.

Cohen, William. "Thomas Jefferson and the Problem of Slavery." *Journal of American History*, Vol. LVI, No. 3 (December 1969), pp. 503–526.

Coolidge, Ellen R. Letter to Joseph Coolidge, Jr., October 24, 1858. Reprinted in the *New York Times*, May 18, 1974.

Dabney, Virginius, and Kukla, Jon. "The Monticello Scandals: History and Fiction." *Virginia Cavalcade*, Vol. XXIX, No. 2 (Autumn 1979), pp. 53–61.

Daniels, Jonathan. *Ordeal of Ambition: Jefferson, Hamilton, Burr*. Garden City: Doubleday, 1970.

Davis, David Brion. *The Problem of Slavery in the Age of Revolution, 1770–1823*. Ithaca: Cornell University Press, 1975.

Donald, David Herbert. "By Sex Obsessed," *Commentary*, Vol. LVII, No. 1 (July 1974), pp. 96–98.

Dos Passos, John. *The Head and Heart of Thomas Jefferson*. Garden City: Doubleday, 1954.

Egan, Clifford. "How Not to Write a Biography: A Critical Look at

Fawn Brodie's *Jefferson.*" *Social Science Journal*, Vol. XIV, No. 2 (April 1977), pp. 129–136.

Farrison, W. Edward. "The Origin of Brown's *Clotel.*" *Phylon*, Vol. XV, December 1954, pp. 347–354.

———. "Clotel, Thomas Jefferson and Sally Hemings." *C.L.A. Journal*, Vol. XVII, No. 2 (December 1971), pp. 147–174.

Fleming, Thomas J. *The Man from Monticello.* New York: William Morrow, 1969.

Flower, Milton E. *James Parton: The Father of Modern Biography.* Durham: Duke University Press, 1951.

Foley, John P., editor. *Jeffersonian Cyclopedia.* New York: Funk and Wagnalls, 1900.

Ford, Paul Leicester, editor. *The Works of Thomas Jefferson* (12 volumes). New York: Putnam, 1904–1905.

Ford, Worthington C., editor. *Thomas Jefferson's Correspondence.* From originals in the collection of William K. Bixby, Boston, 1916.

Furnas, J. C., *Goodbye to Uncle Tom.* New York: William Sloane, 1956.

Graham, Pearl M. "Thomas Jefferson and Sally Hemings." *Journal of Negro History*, Vol. XLIX, No. 2 (April 1961), pp. 89–103.

Hall, Gordon L. *Mr. Jefferson's Ladies.* Boston: Beacon Press, 1966.

Jackson, Luther P. *Free Negro Labor and Property Holding in Virginia, 1830–1960.* New York: Appleton-Century, 1942. Sponsored by American Historical Association.

Jefferson, Thomas. *Notes on the State of Virginia.* William Peden, editor. Chapel Hill: University of North Carolina Press, 1955.

Jeffersonian Cyclopedia, John P. Foley, editor. New York: Funk and Wagnalls, 1900.

Jellison, Charles A. "That Scoundrel Callender." *Virginia Magazine of History and Biography*, Vol. LXVII, No. 3 (July 1959), pp. 295–306.

———. "James Thomson Callender: 'Human Nature in a Hideous Form'." *Virginia Cavalcade*, Vol. XXIX, No. 2 (Autumn 1979), pp. 62–69.

Johnston, James Hugo. *Race Relations in Virginia and Miscegenation in the South, 1776–1860.* Amherst: University of Massachusetts Press, 1970.

Jordan, Winthrop D. *The White Man's Burden: Historical Origins of Racism in the United States.* New York: Oxford University Press, 1974.

―――. *White Over Black: American Attitudes Toward the Negro, 1550–1812.* Chapel Hill: University of North Carolina, 1968. Published for the Institute of Early American History and Culture, Williamsburg, Virginia.

Langhorne, Elizabeth. "The Other Hemings." *Albemarle Magazine,* Vol. III, No. 6 (October–November 1980), pp. 58–66.

Levy, Leonard W. *Jefferson and Civil Liberties: The Darker Side.* Cambridge: Harvard University Press, 1963.

Lewis, Flora. "An Author Ponders Metaphysics of Race." *The New York Times,* October 22, 1979.

Lipscomb and Bergh, editors. *Writings of Thomas Jefferson.* Washington, D.C. 1903.

Logan, Rayford W., editor. *Memoirs of a Monticello Slave.* Charlottesville: University of Virginia Press, 1951.

Malone, Dumas. *Jefferson and His Time* (5 volumes). Boston: Little Brown, 1948, 1951, 1962, 1970, 1974.

――― and Hochman, Steven H. "A Note on Evidence: The Personal History of Madison Hemings." *Journal of Southern History,* Vol. XLI, No. 4 (November 1975), pp. 523–528.

McColley, Robert. *Slavery and Jeffersonian Virginia* (second edition). Urbana: University of Illinois Press, 1973.

Miller, John Chester. *The Wolf by the Ears.* New York: Macmillan, 1977.

Parton, James. *Life of Jefferson.* Boston: James Osgood, 1874.

Peterson, Merrill D. *The Jefferson Image in the American Mind.* New York: Oxford University Press, 1960.

―――. *Thomas Jefferson and the New Nation: A Biography.* New York: Oxford University Press, 1970.

Pierson, Hamilton W. *Jefferson at Monticello.* New York: Charles Scribner, 1862.

Pike County Republican, Waverly, Ohio, March 13 and December 25, 1873.

Randall, Henry S. *The Life of Thomas Jefferson* (3 volumes). Philadelphia: J. B. Lippincott, 1871.

Randolph, Thomas J. "The Last Days of Jefferson." Broadside in University of Virginia Library.

Randolph, Sarah N. *The Domestic Life of Thomas Jefferson* (3rd edition). Charlottesville: Thomas Jefferson Memorial Foundation, 1947.

Richmond Enquirer, 1805.

Richmond Examiner, 1802, 1803.

Richmond Recorder, 1802.

Robinson, Donald L. *Slavery in the Structure of American Politics, 1765–1820.* New York: Harcourt, 1971.

Sandburg, Carl. *Abraham Lincoln: The Prairie Years*, Vol. I. New York: Harcourt, 1926.

Schachner, Nathan. *Thomas Jefferson: A Biography* (2 volumes). New York: Appleton, 1951.

Simmons, Charitey. "Thomas Jefferson: Intimate History, Public Debate." *Chicago Tribune*, July 3, 1979.

Smith, Page. *Jefferson: A Revealing Biography*. New York: American Heritage, 1976.

"Thomas Jefferson's Negro Grandchildren." *Ebony*, Vol. X (November 1954), pp. 78–79.

Trollope, Frances. *Domestic Manners of the Americans*. Michael Sadleir, editor. London: Whittaker, Treacher & Co., 1832.

Van Doren, Carl. *Benjamin Franklin*. New York: Viking Press, 1938.

Van Pelt, Charles B. "Thomas Jefferson and Maria Cosway." *American Heritage*, Vol. XXII, No. 5 (August 1971), pp. 22–29.

Virginia University Magazine, Vol. IV, December 1859, pp. 117–125.

Waverly Watchman, Waverly, Ohio, March 18, 1873.

Wilstach, Paul. "Jefferson's Little Mountain." *National Geographic*, Vol. LV, No. 4 (April 1929), pp. 481–503.

Index

149

About the Author

Virginius Dabney received his B.A. degree in 1920 and his M.A. degree in 1921; both were from the University of Virginia. He was editor of the Richmond *Times-Dispatch* from 1936 to 1969 and was awarded the Pulitzer Prize for his editorials in 1948. He also won the national editorial award twice from Sigma Delta Chi, the Society of Professional Journalists.

At one point in Mr. Dabney's career the Virginia General Assembly became incensed by his newspaper's attacks and called for a state investigation. Mr. Dabney replied that the *Times-Dispatch* would not be "silenced, gagged, or intimidated" by political skulduggery. In 1943, long before civil rights became a burning issue for northern liberals, Mr. Dabney wrote, "The best way to provoke bitter race clashes in this region [the South] over an indefinite period is for whites to turn their backs on the legitimate appeals of the Negroes for justice."

In a lighter vein, Mr. Dabney once conducted a learned and prolonged editorial battle with various areas of the South, but particularly with Kentucky, over the origins, proper method of mixing, and consumption of the mint julep. The winner of this confrontation was never decided.

Mr. Dabney, the recipient of numerous awards and honorary degrees, has lectured at Princeton and Cambridge Universities. He has served as president of the American Society of Newspaper Editors, rector of Virginia Commonwealth University, and chairman of the Virginia Committee on Rhodes Scholarships. He has contributed to a number of publications, including the *Atlantic Monthly, Harper's Magazine, Saturday Review, Foreign Affairs, Saturday Evening Post, Life, American Heritage,* the *Dictionary of American Biography, Encyclopedia Britannica* and the *Economist* of London. He is the author of a dozen books.

Mr. Dabney and his wife live in Richmond.